PEAK TO PEAK SKI TRAILS

OF THE COLORADO FRONT RANGE

by

Harlan N. Barton

Front Range Publishing
889 Forest Avenue, Boulder, Colorado, 80304

Library of Congress Catalog Card No. 89-85887
ISBN: 0-9624606-0-5

Printed by Quality Press, Englewood, Colorado

All photographs by author

Front cover photograph: Sawtooth Mountain from Coney Flats
Back cover photograph: Traverse near Clayton Lake

To Julie for her spirit of adventure

To Jean for loyalty and three fine sons

To Judy for never being dull

CONTENTS

Ski Trails

iii

Illustrations

Bibliography

Index

About the author

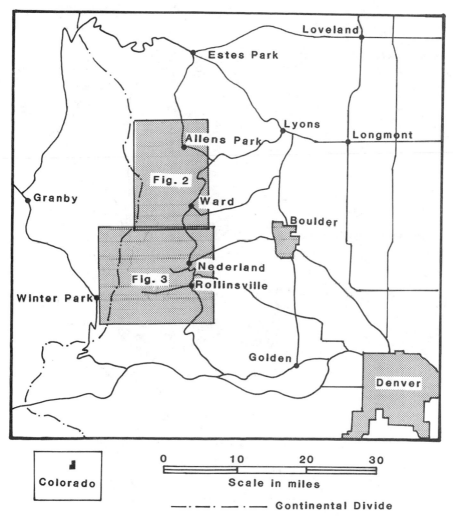

Figure 1

Index map showing location of trail
network maps for north half (figure 2) and
south half (figure 3) of area described by this book.

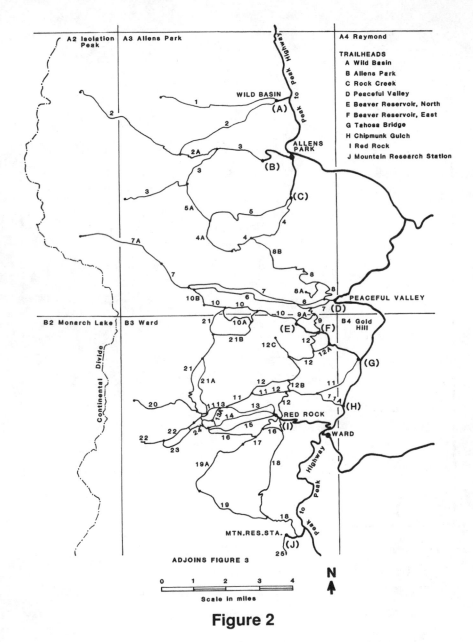

Figure 2

Trail network map showing trails (numbered, some with letter suffixes) and trailheads (lettered and named) on a mosaic of USGS 7.5 minute quadrangle maps for *north* half of area described by this book.

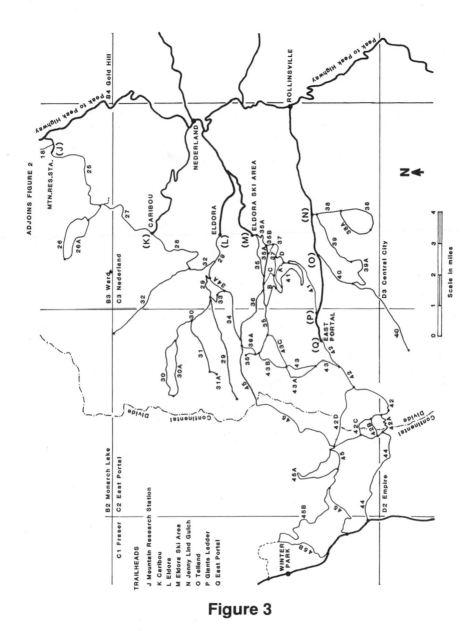

Figure 3

Trail network map showing trails (numbered, some with letter suffixes) and trailheads (lettered and named) on a mosaic of USGS 7.5 minute quadrangle maps for *south* half of area described by this book.

PART ONE INTRODUCTION AND HOW TO USE THIS BOOK

INTRODUCTION

The 87 trails and routes described in this book form a unique two hundred mile network of trails extending from the southern slopes of Mt. Meeker and Longs Peak, thirty miles south along the eastern slope of the Front Range to James Peak. They are bounded by the Peak to Peak Highway on the east and, except for several routes to Winter Park, by the crest of the Front Range which forms the continental divide on the west.

The area is readily accessible from the Denver-Boulder area, with none of the trailheads more than a pleasant one hour drive from Boulder. Access is without the massive traffic jams frequently encountered on week-end trips to western slope skiing on Interstate Highway 70.

State highways and county roads, on easy routes west into the mountains, ascend the valleys of Middle and South St. Vrain Creeks, Left Hand Creek, Middle and South Boulder Creeks, and Coal Creek. These roads end at the north-south Peak to Peak highway which links the mountain communities of Allens Park, Raymond, Peaceful Valley, Ward, Nederland, and Rollinsville. From 18 trailheads, located along this highway or on short spur roads to the west, a web of ski trails extends westward toward the continental divide.

On this network of trails, in addition to out and back trips, numerous combinations of trails of all levels of difficulty can joined into loop trips or skied from one trailhead to another. A note of caution however, many of the routes connecting adjacent trailheads cross from one drainage to another and are consequently not as easy as trails in the valley bottoms. They may not ordinarily offer good snow. They are the best routes between trailheads but the enjoyment may be mainly in the accomplishment. An obvious challenge lies in skiing the entire route from Longs Peak to James Peak.

Trail altitudes range from 8,300 feet at the Wild Basin trailhead to 12,200 feet where several routes cross the divide near Rogers Pass north of James Peak. Altitudes along the continental divide in the area range from 11,671 feet at Rollins Pass to above 13,500 feet at North Arapaho Peak and at Chiefs Head Peak. The eastern side of the divide is precipitous with cirques at the head of glacial valleys along much of the divide. The western side has gentler, tundra covered slopes especially near the southern end of the area considered here.

Heavy forest extending to about 11,000 feet provides shelter from the frequent strong winds out of the west. Above this, the tundra slopes and rock cliffs are exposed to the west wind which transports snow into cornices and hard wind slab, difficult to ski and prone to avalanche, while leaving the windward faces stripped of snow.

Most of the area is administered by federal agencies, although there are islands of private land, some of which are open to skiing. Roosevelt National Forest, administered by the U. S. Forest Service, comprises most of the area. Within Roosevelt National Forest and the adjacent Arapaho National Forest to the west, the Indian Peaks Wilderness takes in most of the higher ground on both sides of the continental divide from Rocky Mountain Park south to Rollins Pass.

High ridge crossing

Wild Basin is within Rocky Mountain National Park and is administered by the National Park Service. The City of Boulder controls the drainage of North Boulder Creek west of Rainbow Lakes road as part of its watershed. This extends south from Niwot Ridge to the east ridge of South Arapaho Peak. Stiff fines have been imposed on those apprehended for trespassing here.

HOW TO USE THIS BOOK

Information on trails is presented in part three and consists of a section on trailheads, trail descriptions for each of the 87 trails, a trail summary table, 20 trail maps, and several smaller scale maps (figures 1-4), showing the network of trails and their relationship to towns, roads, U.S. Geological Survey (USGS) maps and trail maps.

Trailheads

Directions for driving to each of the eighteen trailheads from the nearest of four mountain towns in the area (Allens Park, Ward, Nederland, or Rollinsville) are given in a separate trailhead section in part three.

Trail descriptions and trail summary table

The 87 trail descriptions and the trail summary table both present information on access, difficulty and other trail characteristics in a standardized format that facilitates access to specific information. Each trail description discusses a trail's characteristics in detail whereas the trail summary table presents information in a condensed format that allows comparison amongst trails. Much of the information about a trail is presented in both formats, but each format contains some information not found in the other.

Most information presented in the trail descriptions is self-explanatory, that in the trail summary table is less so due primarily to the extensive use of abbreviations and numerical ratings. The following paragraphs explain some of the conventions and definitions used in both.

Trail numbers indicate the classification of a trail as a main trail (no suffix) or as a sub-trail (A, B, C, etc. suffix). Of the 87 trails, 45 are classified as main trails and 42 are classified as sub-trails. The distinction is somewhat arbitrary, generally a main trail is one that would constitute a ski trip by itself while sub-trails may be spurs off a main trail, extensions of a main trail, connections between trails, or alternates to a main trail. Trails are numbered from north to south.

Trail names were selected to conform as near as possible with those shown on USGS topographic maps, Forest Service maps, trail signs, and other publications. There are, however a few cases where there are contradictions among these. Where no name existed, a trail name was originated incorporating the name of a nearby topographic or cultural feature. Trail names commonly include the term *Trail* implying that a recognizable trail exists. When *Route* is used as part of the name, no definite path exists. Routes represent a general line of travel from one point to another. A ridge, drainage, direction, or a line on a map may represent a route. In a few cases, *Road* may be part of the trail name and in one instance, *Railroad Grade.*

USGS maps, 7.5 minute, (scale 1:24,000) are referenced in the text by both the USGS quadrangle name and by an abbreviated letter/number name from which the position of a map relative to adjacent ones is apparent. Only the

Winter wonderland

3

abbreviation is used in the trail summary table. The following diagram, on which north is toward the top, shows the configuration of USGS maps for the area and gives both the USGS and the abbreviated names.

DIAGRAM OF USGS MAPS FOR AREA

	1	2	3	4
A	—	Isolation Peak (A2)	Allens Park (A3)	Raymond (A4)
B	—	Monarch Lake (B2)	Ward (B3)	Gold Hill (B4)
C	Fraser (C1)	East Portal (C2)	Nederland (C3)	—
D	—	Empire (D2)	Central City (D3)	—

By way of example, the USGS Nederland quadrangle map is abbreviated as C3, Ward is B3, East Portal is C2. With familiarity with the system, it can be deduced without need for reference to the diagram that Map B3 is north of Map C3 or that Map C1 is west of Map C2, etc.,.

Trail maps are referenced in text and table by map number. Locations of the 87 trails are shown on 20 maps.

Trail characteristics such as the overall difficulty rating are described for each trail using a consistent set of terms (easy, moderate, moderate-difficult, difficult, very difficult). The trail summary table presents similar information, but uses numerical ratings on a scale of 1 to 5. The terms used in the trail descriptions and the corresponding numerical ratings used in the trail summary table for various characteristics are given in the following index.

INDEX OF TRAIL CHARACTERISTICS

Difficulty, overall
1. Easy
2. Moderate
3. Moderate-difficult
4. Difficult
5. Very difficult

Technical skiing skill, Routefinding skill
1. Novice
2. Beginner
3. Intermediate
4. Advanced
5. Expert

Endurance
1. Very easy
2. Easy
3. Moderate
4. Strenuous
5. Very strenuous

Snow quality
1. Very poor
2. Poor
3. Medium
4. Good
5. Excellent

Amount of use
1. Nearly unused
2. Very light
3. Light
4. Moderate
5. Heavy

Gradient or steepness
1. Nearly flat
2. Slight
3. Moderate
4. Steep
5. Very steep

Nearing the continental divide

Trail type describes trails in the trail summary table as either (Rd) road, (JR) jeep road, (Tr) trail, or (Rt) route. The distinction is not exact but defines characteristics that can usually be distinguished with snow cover. A road frequently has cut-banks, less sharp curves, and is wider than a jeep road. Jeep roads are usually wider than trails but may be difficult to recognize in scattered trees if untracked. The distinction between trails and routes was presented in the *Trail name* paragraph.

Difficulty rating and the associated specific skills recommended for a particular trail are discussed in the trail text descriptions and are presented in columns 5 through 9 of the trail summary table. The overall difficulty of a trail is a combination of the specific skills recommended. It represents the difficulty expected under normal conditions. For example, on an above timberline route where high winds and wind-sculptured snow are common, the difficulty rating reflects these conditions. The rating is given for skiing the entire route. Frequently the beginning part of a trail is easier and should be considered if one is looking for a shorter and less difficult trip.

Technical skiing skill recommended for a trip indicates what skill is necessary to ski the specified terrain under the expected snow conditions. It does not consider distance, total altitude gain or loss, weather, or remoteness from trailheads.

Endurance rating reflects both the length and the altitude gain and loss of a trail. Considered also is the expected snow quality, the probability of having to break trail, and the length of the connecting trails which provide access.

Route-finding skill is a measure of the skill and equipment (maps, compass, altimeter, etc.) which may be necessary to follow the route. It varies from simply following tracks on a blazed trail through closely-spaced trees to traveling untracked routes above or below timberline in bad weather and reduced visibility.

Survival and mountaineering skill is a product of the difficulty of the terrain, altitude, remoteness from the trailhead, amount of use on the route, expected snow conditions, and probable exposure to adverse weather. It is, in addition to a measure of recommended skill, an indication of preparation, equipment, and clothing which is appropriate. It is given in the table only.

Trail through aspen grove

Snow quality is an estimate of the quality of the snow pack that

6

would be encountered during mid-winter under normal conditions. It is subjective, based on the author's experience in skiing most of the trails a number of times. Those trails with a higher rating, in addition to offering better snow under normal conditions, have a longer season.

Amount of use is an estimate of the amount of use to be expected on a given trail. It is also subjective. A rating of 1 indicates the trail is nearly unused, a rating of 5 indicates very heavy use. Nothing is entirely without its shortcomings however, a corollary of light usage is a high probability of breaking trail. One of the benefits hopefully to be derived from this guide book is to point out some less used but interesting trails with good snow. Other ways of avoiding crowded conditions are to start early and ski further from the trailhead.

Wind exposure is presented in the trail summary table as an estimate of the percentage of the length of the trail significantly exposed to wind. Trail descriptions point out wind exposed localities.

Skiing time, out and back, is given for an intermediate skier without allowance of time for stops. An approximation of the sustained speed of an intermediate skier with a day pack over mountainous terrain of different gradients is:

Up	steep gradient	1.2 mi/hr
Up	moderate gradient	1.7 mi/hr
—	level gradient	2.0 mi/hr
Down	moderate gradient	2.7 mi/hr
Down	steep gradient	3.5 mi/hr

Altitude gain and loss in both the text descriptions and trail summary table columns are in feet and are cumulative for the gain and loss columns. Commonly gain and loss pertain to a trip outbound from a trailhead. For a trip from one trailhead to another, the starting trailhead may be determined from the text description.

Gradient is given in the trail summary table for both the average steepness or that which is frequently encountered and for the maximum steepness encountered. Trail descriptions locate steep sections.

Maps

Four figures or maps of smaller scale show the coverage and relative positions of the twenty large scale trail maps.

Consulting guidebook and notes

7

Figure 1 shows the location of the area covered by the two trail network maps (figures 2 and 3) relative to the cities and towns of the region.

Figures 2 and 3 show the network of trails for the northern and southern halves of the area respectively. Areal coverage of the USGS 7.5 minute quadrangle maps is shown along with locations of the 18 trailheads and the mountain communities.

Figure 4 shows the coverage of the 20 trail maps relative to USGS 7.5 minute quadrangle maps.

Trail maps show detailed traces of the 87 trails on 20 maps. Each trail map is a reproduction of a quarter of a USGS 7.5 minute quadrangle map. North is at the top of all maps and all are at the same scale (approximately 1:42,000). Numbers (with or without letter suffixes) appearing beside the trails designate the trail number. Trail distances are not given on the maps to avoid confusion due to the interwoven nature of the trails, but are given instead in the trail descriptions. Names and letter abbreviations designate trailheads on the maps. The magnetic declination averages 13.5 degrees East.

PART TWO GENERAL INFORMATION

Reporting emergencies

Search and rescue is the responsibility of the county sheriff. Most of the area covered in this book is within Boulder County except for trails originating along South Boulder Creek in Gilpin County, and the trails to Winter Park on the western side of the continental divide in Grand County. After requests for aid are processed by the sheriffs department, mountain rescue is generally performed by the Rocky Mountain Rescue Group. Located in Boulder, this volunteer organization was founded in 1947.

To report emergencies: (1) call the sheriff, (2) describe the problem and ask that a Rescue Group mission leader call you back, (3) remain at the telephone so that the mission leader can speak with you directly.

Call the following numbers to reach the Boulder County sheriff from:

Allens Park, Raymond, Peaceful Valley 747-2538
Ward 459-3436
Nederland 258-3232
Boulder 911

Call the following number to reach the Gilpin County sheriff from:

Nederland, Rollinsville 258-3956

Pay telephones are at the following locations: (1) In Raymond at the fire station across the road from the Raymond store, (2) At the Millsite Inn, 0.3 miles north of Ward, (3) In Ward at the fire station, (4) In Nederland at the main bus stop in Wolftounge Square, (5) At Eldora Ski Area in the lodge, (6) In Rollinsville at both the Stage Stop Inn and at the liquor store. All are outside except (5). Coins are required to reach the toll-free sheriff's numbers.

Weather, avalanche, and road condition information sources

Toll-free recorded messages may be heard from a number of sources. The U. S. Forest Service and the Colorado Avalanche Information Center at 236-9435 provide information on weather, snow conditions, and avalanche hazards. The Colorado State Patrol at 639-1111 presents information on road conditions. Colorado Ski Country at 831-7669 reports information at downhill ski areas, including: new snow, depth of base, surface conditions, and weather. Eldora ski area at 440-8800 provides snow and weather conditions. The National Weather Service at 398-3964 provides a weather forecast for the Denver area.

Tracks in deep powder

Skiing with organized groups

Several organizations conduct ski tours led by persons familiar with the area. The most active is the Colorado Mountain Club (CMC) with large groups in Boulder and Denver, smaller groups in nearby Loveland, Longmont, Fort Collins, and Estes Park, and in other locations throughout the state. On a typical weekend in midwinter the Boulder group will conduct about four ski tours with many located in the area described by this book. The Denver group will have probably twice that number but scattered throughout a larger area. The club also schedules snowshoe trips and extensive hiking and climbing activities, summer and winter. Information may be obtained by calling the state and Denver group offices at 922-8315 or the Boulder group at 449-1135.

The Flatirons Ski Club in Boulder places more emphasis on downhill skiing, but nonetheless schedules cross country trips. These are generally more socially oriented than the CMC trips.

The Sierra Club chapter in Boulder schedules a limited number of outings.

9

Public transportation

The Denver-Boulder public transit system (RTD) provides bus service to Eldora Ski Area from Boulder. The regional fare from Boulder or Denver is $2.50 during the 1989-90 season.

Return transportation to Denver from an across the divide trip to Winter Park can be by bus or train. Call Greyhound/Trailways at 292-6111 for fare and schedule information. The ski train from Denver Union Station to Winter Park is operated by ANSCO. It runs only on Saturdays and Sundays. Call Ticket Master at 290-8497 for information, reservations, and tickets.

Ski-in-huts

Two huts are operated by the Boulder Group of the Colorado Mountain Club. A cabin near Brainard Lake is available for overnight use by members of any group of the CMC and their guests for a fee. The cabin is locked and reservations are required. All persons are welcome to stop for a rest and hot drink for a small fee when the cabin is hosted on week-ends. The Arestua Hut near the top of Guinn Mountain is open without reservations. Cooking with backpacking stoves is not allowed in either hut due to the extreme danger of fire and the disastrous consequences of what might start as a minor fire. Cooking can be done on the wood-burning stoves in each. A third hut, the Pfiffner Hut near Rogers Pass Lake, was removed during the summer of 1988 as no longer serviceable.

The Estes Park Group of the CMC serves hot drinks on week-ends at a warming hut near the Wild Basin Trailhead.

The Tennessee Mountain Cabin operated by the Eldora Ski Area is on their fee trail system.

Safety

Serious or life threatening situations in backcountry skiing are largely from two sources, avalanche and hypothermia.

Avalanche statistics place Colorado as the most dangerous state, recording 103 deaths from avalanche in a 37 year period beginning in 1950. This is more than twice that of second place Washington, according to Knox Williams, director of the Colorado Avalanche Information Center. Avalanche avoidance is a matter of education, awareness, and prudence so that areas likely to

Rest stop

run are avoided during periods of instability. Avalanche rescue rests almost entirely upon the resources of a backcountry ski group. Avalanche transceivers, shovels, and a party large enough to effect an immediate search and rescue effort are necessary. A skier alone has little chance of surviving burial in an avalanche.

Hypothermia can result from being forced to bivouac due to any or a combination of several reasons; becoming lost, equipment failure, physical injury, or deteriorating weather coupled with poor judgement about capabilities. Becoming lost can be avoided by learning better routefinding skills, having maps and compass, and most of all, by giving the necessary attention to routefinding. The consequences of equipment failure can usually be avoided by carrying repair and replacement tools and equipment. A reliable headlamp can at times enable one to avoid a bivouac by skiing out in darkness. Equipment repair and headlamps are discussed in the equipment section.

Survival in a bivouac situation may well depend on the clothing and bivouac equipment carried and on having informed a reliable person about your plans. This person should have been instructed to call the county sheriff at a specified time on your failure to return and have been provided with information identifying the car used, where it would be parked, the planned route along with possible alternatives, and the expected time of return. Given this information, the chances of rescue that night or the following day are good in most cases.

Skiing alone decreases the ability to deal with some hazards, such as avalanche rescue or the ability to send for help in case of physical injury. Skiing with companions is not a panacea however. They may serve only to make the party less decisive.

Light frostbite of the face, common when exposed to wind, can be avoided or minimized by periodically checking companions faces for white spots and warming these by hand.

Litter

Few people today participating in cross country skiing discard the conventional litter of orange peels, plastic bags, or toilet tissue. Some unthinkingly do leave sticky wax scrapings in the trail. A few think it necessary to leave the brightly colored flagging or surveyors tape to mark a trail already adequately marked by blue diamond markers. Trail markings are not allowed in wilderness areas and flagging wouldn't seem to be necessary elsewhere with the majority of trails well marked with tree blazes or otherwise apparent. Leave something to discover for those who follow. I pick up these unsightly scraps the same as other litter.

Private property

Private property restrictions are noted in each trail description when they were encountered. Restrictions and postings change with time however, so do not consider the absence of restrictions mentioned here as constituting permission to ski on private property. Obey posted signs.

Dogs

Dogs are not allowed on trails in Rocky Mountain National Park, on the Waldrop (North), CMC South, and Little Raven Trails from Red Rock Trailhead to Brainard Lake, and on the Jenny Creek Forest Access Trail through the Eldora Ski Area.

Route finding

The necessity for routefinding, navigation or orienteering skills in backcountry ski touring varies greatly. Little skill is required to follow a tracked trail cut through stands of closely spaced timber and blazed with blue diamond markers compared to that necessary in following an indistinct route above timberline or through thick timber in a white-out or darkness. Even the seemingly foolproof technique of following tracks can pose problems, as there is no guarantee that tracks alone mean a trail. They may mean only that an off-trail skier wandered this way. Tracks are also at times very temporary, being subject to obliteration in a few minutes by wind or in little more time by new snowfall. A skier can be deprived of even his own tracks for a return route.

Other indicators of an established trail are more permanent, tree clearing and trimming of branches is apparent in dense timber but less so in more widely spaced trees. The traditional inverted "!" tree slash or the flattened metal can nailed to a tree mark some trails but these are being replaced by the more visible blue diamond trail markers. Some of these, slightly darker than others, appear almost black through amber sun glasses and are consequently less noticeable. Contrary to their meaning at downhill ski areas, they indicate nothing about the difficulty rating of the trail. Trails in Rocky Mountain Park are often marked with orange square blazes. Trails within the Indian Peaks Wilderness are unmarked except for old and frequently indistinct tree slashes.

Trail signs are surprisingly impermanent. They suffer the effects of the elements, nibbling horses, vandalism, souvenir seekers, and the vagaries of the Forest Service. Another form of trail marking is the use of cairns above timberline. The Rollins Pass route is marked part of the way by an abandoned telegraph pole line. Flagging, the brightly colored surveyors tape has been discussed in the section on litter. Its only justifiable use is in an emergency or to mark a route temporarily. Then it should be tied shoe lace fashion so that it may be removed with a single pull on the return trip.

U.S. Geological Survey 7.5 minute quadrangle maps at a scale of 1:24,000 and in six colors present information that is not entirely retained on maps reproduced in guidebooks in a single color and at smaller scales. Four of these maps (Allens Park, Ward, Nederland, and East Portal) cover the majority of the trails discussed in this book. Trimming or folding back half of the margins (top and left on each map) to the neat line aids in seeing the continuity of terrain features across map boundaries. A consistent system of folding has advantages in storage and viewing, in addition to lessening damage from repeated folding in different places. After trimming the right boundary to near the neat line but retaining the marginal information and folding the bottom margin under, a single vertical fold down the center followed by accordion folds into four sections yields a map which can be viewed in its entirety with a folded size of six by nine inches, small enough to fit into a parka pocket or fanny pack. An accessible map which can be consulted frequently including when weather conditions are extreme is of far greater use than a map buried in a pack. A plastic map cover, trimmed to size and open on two sides provides protection from both snow and from crumpling in the pocket or pack, while allowing easy access to change the accordion section which is visible.

A simple compass with a rectangular transparent body having provision for an attachment cord and with a graduated rotating azimuth ring is well suited for winter use. Map orientation and the ability to follow a selected compass course by centering the needle over an arrow are the major uses. Like the map, it should always be accessible even though clothing changes may have to be made to accommodate to changing weather conditions. It may be attached with a neck loop or to clothing with a cord and alligator clamp. Once a compass direction has been established, shadows if present, may be used to maintain a given direction with sufficient precision for most situations.

An altimeter can be extremely useful in determining ones position along a linear terrain feature such as a valley, trail or ridge when visibility is restricted by trees, snow, or darkness. It should be reset frequently to minimize the transfers of distance, altitude and time. Notes made prior to a trip of altitudes of key points along the route assist in gauging progress toward them and facilitates resetting the altimeter as they are passed.

The altimeter may also be used as a barometer to assist in weather prediction. Verification of the calibration for this purpose is done at home or other place of known altitude when the current barometric pressure is known. The altimeter is made to show both the current barometric pressure and altitude. The Thommen altimeter can be adjusted to do this with a jewelers screwdriver through a small hole in the backside.

Other useful aids are a watch, pocket size notebook, and pencil. The usefulness of information such as time traveled on various segments of the trip as well as landmark information is usually not recognized until later in the trip. Then it often isn't possible to be accurately recalled unless it was recorded. A wood pencil is reliable and avoids the hassle of trying to write with a frozen ball point pen or load a mechanical pencil in a high wind with freezing fingers.

Equipment

For skiing trails or routes classified as difficult or very difficult, special equipment and clothing aids in adapting to conditions of steep terrain, difficult snow conditions, high wind, severe weather, high altitude, greater trail distances, and more remote location. Maps, compass, and altimeter have already been discussed in the routefinding section.

Travelers above timberline or along open meadows or lakes, should have face protection readily accessible for use. Long gaiters necessary to keep snow out of boots and off socks in breaking trail, prevent heat loss in the wind above timberline. Special aids to difficult skiing conditions include metal edged skis, heavy duty boots, climbing skins affixed with adhesive, and a pack with ski-carrying slots in the event walking becomes necessary. Avalanche rescue equipment may include avalanche transceivers, ski pole avalanche probes, and shovels. Material and tools to repair or replace broken poles, bindings, wooden

ski tips, torn or separated boots, lost baskets, and binding parts and screws should be carried. These include nylon alpine cord, wire, duct tape, nylon strapping tape, selected screws and small bolts and nuts, swiss army knife and pliers. Split sections of plastic pipe and hose clamps make a repair kit for poles. A second water bottle for long trips is advisable as is foam insulation to prevent its contents from freezing. Plastic trash bags are a lightweight aid in keeping clothing dry in a snow bivouac.

A headlamp can allow one to continue skiing after dark instead of huddling in a snow shelter. No trip of more than a few miles should be undertaken without one. An excellent but heavy headlamp is powered with four alkaline D cells. Modification may be necessary to insure that good electrical contact is maintained

Bracing against wind on continental divide

even when subjected to shaking. Accidental turn on in the pack should be prevented by modification or reversing batteries. Steel wool for cleaning contacts and a spare bulb should be carried. Used only when necessary and with use on the trail shared with companions, the four alkaline D cells will last an incredible time. When a lighter headlamp with less battery capacity is used, spare batteries should be routinely carried.

Skiing difficult conditions

Much of the eastern slope offers snow of excellent quality. However, weather conditions characteristic of the eastern slope of the Rockies in comparison to the western slope include higher temperatures, less snowfall, and most importantly, high winds. These can combine to produce snow conditions on exposed steep slopes that are difficult to ski.
Mastery of the advanced techniques of cross country skiing, telemark and parallel, aids in the enjoyable skiing of a variety of snow conditions; deep powder, heavy wet snow, wind slab, and variable breakable crust, over steep terrain. Less aesthetic snow plow and step turns are still valuable techniques for steep packed trails. Instruction is available from ski schools, the Colorado Mountain Club, or private individuals.

Devious, or what some purists might consider unethical, methods of coping with or even avoiding difficult conditions should not be overlooked. Falling may be part of the process of learning advanced technique, but excessive falling and the resultant struggle to regain ones feet is exhausting. Each fall then contributes to additional falls.

Techniques of controlling speed include dragging ski pole baskets in the loose snow on the side of the trail and of straddling poles with the points dug in. Climbing skins can be used for slowing the descent although this results in the loss of edge control and contributes significantly to their wear. Contrary to what some comedians suggest, they are not put on backward for really steep descents.

Skiing unpacked snow along the edge of a packed trail aids in controlling speed while maintaining good form. On an untracked steep trail, the first person down goes the slowest while those following have the advantage of seeing where the bumps are. Steep icy trail sections may sometimes be detoured by gentle traverses through the trees linked by kick turns. The burning sensation in the upper leg muscles from long snowplow descents on steep packed trails may be relieved by relaxing the stance periodically and letting the skis run. For snowplowing steep packed trails across a slope, hold the upper ski straight ahead and the lower ski at an extreme angle. Short steep sections of a packed trail may be descended by sideslipping or by sidestepping.

Extremely hard windslab above timberline, either smooth or sculptured by the wind into sastrugi can sometimes be negotiated better by walking than skiing. The practicality depends on the extent of the hardpacked snow. The same is true for hard or icy sections of trail with exposed rocks at lower altitudes. Trails should not be walked however, where the snow is not strong enough to prevent postholing.

Rotation of the lead in breaking trail aids in conserving strength. It is accomplished without interrupting progress by the leader stepping aside after an interval of leading, and waiting for the entire group to pass.

Rollins Pass ogre

Particularly unfavorable snow conditions, especially the mixed conditions found near or above timberline can sometimes be more easily dealt with on snowshoes. Although lacking the speed and thrill of the descent of skis, the newer Sherpa style snowshoe is a marvel of reliability and effectiveness for these conditions.

Finally one can try to ski the best snow available. The main criteria are simple; trees, altitude, and north-facing. Trees, large and dense enough to provide shelter from sun and wind are probably the most important factor affecting snow quality on the eastern slope. Nearly as important and interrelated, is altitude. Without the protection of trees, above timberline slopes are, except immediately following a snowfall, exposed to the deleterious effects of wind. Slopes on the windward side of ridges are blown clear of snow which is deposited as cornices and hard wind slab snowfields on the leeward side. The snow surface may sculptured by the wind into sastrugi.

The best snow will be as high as there is good tree cover. Snow from 10,000 feet to timberline is always better than that found lower. There is more snowfall at the higher altitude and temperatures remain colder. Although mitigated by good tree cover, the effect of sun on a south-facing slope degrades the snow more rapidly than on a north-facing one. Finally a trail with less traffic will have better snow where other conditions are equal.

Open slopes above timberline

Weather forecasting

Most ski trips in the front range are short and weather prediction is not normally necessary if a forecast has been obtained prior to starting the trip. Telephone numbers for obtaining this information are given in the *Information sources* section. The following rules of thumb however, may add to ones skill in short range forecasting and enjoyment. They are from the CompuServe Outdoor Forum, a public domain source and were reprinted in Newsletter vol. 1, #3, of the Tenth Mountain Trail Association.

1. Steadily falling barometric pressure usually means an approaching storm while steadily rising pressure signals clearing weather. An altimeter allows you to evaluate this and number 2.

2. There is little chance of precipitation continuing when the barometric pressure is more than 30.10.

3. When the temperature during a storm drops to less than 5 degrees F, snowfall will rapidly diminish.

4. Cirrus clouds can precede a storm by 24 hours or more. A ring around the moon is caused by thin cirrus.

5. Mountain wave clouds and snow plumes on ridges, indicate high winds at mountain top levels.

6. Frontal passage (the end of a storm) is often indicated by the lowest point of the barometric pressure curve (you can plot this from your altimeter), a wind shift, and a sudden appearance of heavily rimed snow crystals or graupel.

7. If the wind direction changes clockwise with time (for example, wind out of the south changing to the west), expect mostly fair weather; low pressure is passing to the north. If the wind direction turns counterclockwise (northwest becoming southwest), expect poor weather; low pressure is passing to the south.

8. Current weather reports on radio, especially NOAA Weather Radio on VHF band (162.55 MHz, Denver and 162.40 MHz, Sterling), are your best sources for accurate forecasts while skiing.

PART THREE TRAIL INFORMATION

TRAILHEADS

Each of the 87 trails described in this book begins at one of the 18 trailheads listed here or branches from trails that do. Directions to the start of a given trail are presented in the *Access* section of that trail description and consist of a reference to one of the trailheads identified by name and a letter abbreviation. Access is further described where necessary, by identifying connecting trails and the distance skied from the trailhead. Trailhead information is presented in an abbreviated form in the trail summary table where the trailhead is identified only by the letter abbreviation.

Directions on how to reach each trailhead from the nearest of four towns are given here. The towns—Allens Park, Ward, Nederland, and Rollinsville—are familiar to most residents of the Denver-Boulder area or can be located with a road map. Mileage from Allens Park is given from the northernmost of the two exits from Highway 7. From Ward, mileage is given from the junction of the Left Hand Canyon road with Highway 72. Mileage from Nederland, unless specified differently is from the RTD bus stop in Wolftongue Square in the center of town. Mileage from Rollinsville is from the junction of the East Portal road with Highway 119.

A. **Wild Basin Trailhead**. (Alt. 8,360 ft., Map 3) From Allens Park, drive north 2.1 miles on Highway 7, turn left (west) onto a loop road toward the Wild Basin Ranger Station. Drive 0.4 miles to the parking area on the right side of the road, about 100 yards beyond the Wild Basin Lodge.

B. **Allens Park Trailhead**. (Alt. 8,900 ft., Map 3) Exit Highway 7 at the northernmost of the two Allens Park exits, drive south one block to the corner with both the Allens Park Community Church and post office, and turn right onto the road heading west. At 0.8 miles from the corner take the left (more prominent) fork and continue on the curving, climbing road to the trailhead at 1.4 miles. Here at a summer parking lot at the boundary of Rocky Mountain Park, the trailhead is marked with a sign *Allens Park Trail.*

C. **Rock Creek Trailhead**. (Alt. 8,580 ft., Map 6) Exit Highway 7 at the northernmost of the two Allens Park exits, drive south one block to the corner with both the Allens Park Community Church and post office, turn left to go east one block and turn right at the road sign *Ski Road, County Road 107.* Drive south 1.4 miles to where snow conditions generally make further driving inadvisable. Park at the edge of the road.

D. **Peaceful Valley Trailhead**. (Alt. 8,520 ft., Map 6) From Ward, drive north 5.8 miles on Highway 72. Park on the plowed loop road on the west side or on the edge of the highway where it makes a curve to the west to cross Middle St. Vrain Creek.

From Lyons, drive west on Highway 7 up the canyon of South and Middle St. Vrain Creeks 13.9 miles to the junction with Highway 72, then south on Highway 72, 3.9 miles.

E. **Beaver Reservoir North Trailhead**. (Alt. 9,190 ft., Map 8) From Ward, drive north 2.5 miles on Highway 72, turn west onto the forest access road, pass Camp Tahosa, and continue on to Beaver Reservoir. Follow the road around the lake, across a concrete spillway to the trail sign at 2.6 miles from the highway turnoff.

F. **Beaver Reservoir East Trailhead**. (Alt. 9,140 ft., Map 8) The directions are the same as for Beaver Reservoir North, but stop 2.0 miles from the highway turnoff, or 300 yards before the lake, where trail signs are visible on both sides of the road.

G. **Tahosa Bridge Trailhead**. (Alt. 8,740 ft., Map 9) From Ward, drive north 2.5 miles on Highway 72 and turn west onto the same forest access road as for Beaver Reservoir North and East. Immediately cross a bridge and park on the far side near the trail sign for the South St. Vrain Trail.

H. **Chipmunk Gulch Trailhead**. (Alt. 9,190 ft., Map 9) From Ward, drive north 0.9 miles on Highway 72 to a road-cut. Park on the side of the highway.

I. **Red Rock Trailhead**. (Alt. 10,060 ft., Map 8) From Ward, drive north on Highway 72 200 yards, turn west on the Brainard Lake road and continue 2.6 miles to the end of the plowed road. The trailhead area has a winter closure vehicle gate, numerous trail signs, and parking along the edge of the road.

J. **Mountain Research Station Trailhead**. (Alt. 9,290 ft., Map 11) From Ward, drive south on Highway 72, 4.7 miles to a sign *University of Colorado Research Station.* Drive west on this road past a sign marking the Sourdough Trail at 0.5 miles. The road is too narrow for parking here so continue on to a curve at 0.9 miles where space is generally plowed for parking. Here the unplowed road to the left continues to Rainbow Lakes and the plowed road to the right to the research station.

The turnoff from the highway may also be reached by driving north from Nederland 7.0 miles on Highway 72.

K. **Caribou Trailhead.** (Alt. 9,990 ft., Map 13) From Nederland, start northbound on Highway 72 and while still in town, turn off to the left at a sign for Caribou. Drive 5.4 miles west from this junction, past the turnoffs to the Cross Mountain and Caribou Silver Mines and past the stone building ruins marking the townsite of Caribou. Continue optionally up the rocky and steeper road to the top of the saddle and trailhead.

I have always found this road plowed, presumably by one of the mining operators, and passable with a passenger car. The county road department does not maintain it for passenger cars nor provide snow removal. Obviously one should not depend on it being plowed to get out if heavy snowfall or high winds occur.

L. **Eldora Trailhead.** (Alt. 8,810 ft., Map 13) From Nederland, start southbound on Highway 72 and at the edge of town, turn off to the right at the sign for Eldora Ski Area. Follow this paved road west, past a turnoff to the ski area at 1.4 miles from the highway, and continue up the valley bottom through Eldora to the end of the plowed road at the far edge of town at 3.9 miles. Park along the designated side of the road.

M. **Eldora Ski Area Trailhead.** (Alt. 9,360 ft., Map 13) From Nederland, start southbound on Highway 72 and at the edge of town, turn right at the ski area sign. Take the left fork at 1.4 miles which climbs out of the valley to the ski area at 4.2 miles. Park in the first parking lot, near the base of a wide beginners slope with a short chair lift and the ski area's cross country ticket and information booth.

RTD, the Denver-Boulder metropolitan area public transit system, has bus service to the ski area. A one-way fare from Boulder or Denver is $2.50 for the 1989-90 season.

N. **Jenny Lind Gulch Trailhead.** (Alt. 8,800 ft., Map 17) From Rollinsville, drive west on the road paralleling and to the north of the railroad, toward East Portal. Parking at the trailhead is designated by signs along the road at 3.8 miles.

O. **Tolland Trailhead.** (Alt. 8,920 ft., Map 17) From Rollinsville, drive west on the road paralleling and to the north of the railroad, toward East Portal. Pass the Jenny Lind Gulch trailhead and continue 0.1 mile past Tolland to where an unplowed road forks off uphill to the left at 5.2 miles. Park at the edge of the road.

P. **Giants Ladder Trailhead.** (Alt. 9,190 ft., Map 16) From Rollinsville, drive west toward East Portal, passing the Jenny Lind Gulch and Tolland trailheads. The trailhead is at a sign-marked junction with the old railroad grade on the right at 7.2 miles. Snowmobilers are frequently here. Park at the edge of the road.

Q. **East Portal Trailhead**. (Alt. 9,210 ft., Map 16) From Rollinsville, drive west on the road paralleling and to the north of the railroad. Continue 8.0 miles to the end of the road at East Portal and the Moffat Tunnel. Observe the parking restrictions near the tunnel.

R. **Brainard Lake Trailhead**. (Alt. 10,345 ft., Map 7) This is not a true trailhead as it is not accessible by vehicle. For convenience, it is treated as one in the trail descriptions and in the trail summary table because it is the starting point for several trails which go beyond it and access to it is by any of several other trails.

From Red Rock Trailhead, ski west on the CMC South Trail (15), 2.0 miles to Brainard Lake. Add 0.5 mile to ski to the west side of the lake on the Brainard Loop Road (14 A) and an additional 0.4 mile to reach either the Mitchell or Long Lake trails by the Mitchell Lake Road Spur (14 B) or Long Lake Road Spur (14 C).

Brainard Lake may also be reached from Red Rock Trailhead by either the Waldrop North Trail (13), Brainard Lake Road (14), or Little Raven Trail (16) with only a slight increase in distance traveled.

SKI TRAILS

TRAIL NO. 1

SANDBEACH LAKE TRAIL

TRAIL MAPS: 3, 2

SUMMARY

This infrequently used summer hiking trail nearly always offers excellent snow on the ascent out of Wild Basin onto the forested southern slopes of Mt. Meeker. First you must climb a steep south-facing slope from the trailhead to the top of Copeland Moraine. This slope may be without snow due to the effects of sun and wind at low altitude. Thereafter the trail is protected and the gradient generally moderate. Unobstructed views from Sandbeach Lake reveal the distant Indian Peaks beyond the rim of Wild Basin as well as the nearby imposing mass of Mt. Meeker.

CLASSIFICATION: Difficult

MAPS (USGS 7.5' quadrangles)

Allens Park (A3)

ELEVATIONS (feet)

Starting....................................8,360
Highest...................................10,330
Cumulative gain 2,010
Cumulative loss...........................40

DISTANCE (miles, one way).......4.2

TIME (hours)

Outbound 3.2
Return 1.7

ACCESS

At Wild Basin trailhead (A).

USAGE

Very light, many skiers are probably discouraged from attempting this trail by the usual lack of snow at Copeland Lake and on the steep, frequently exposed grassy slopes above.

SNOW CONDITIONS

Snow conditions are usually very poor at the start due to the low altitude and exposure of the treeless south-facing slope to the impact of sun and wind. Conditions improve dramatically on reaching the shelter of trees at the top of Copeland Moraine at 9,000 feet altitude and 1.2 miles, and continue to improve with the steady gain in altitude thereafter.

WIND EXPOSURE

Trees shelter the entire trail except for the initial 1.2 miles and at Sandbeach Lake.

GRADIENT

The steepness of the abrupt climb of 200 feet in the initial 300 yards on the older trail is lessened by the longer switchbacks of the new. Thereafter the gradient is generally moderate but constant except for a short steep section beyond Hunters Creek at 3.2 miles.

ROUTE DESCRIPTION

From a large sign at the trailhead parking area, a recently constructed unblazed trail climbs 150 yards northeast to switchback left onto a long climbing traverse west through massive Ponderosa Pines, interrupted by one 30 yard switchback. Orange square blazes at 100 to 400 yard intervals mark the trail after the initial 0.4 miles.

Alternatively, the trail may be begun 150 yards to the west near the northeast corner of Copeland Lake. Here, faded orange square blazes mark an older trail that climbs more directly up the steep slope to the north over giant steps of logs emplaced to prevent erosion. The new trail is joined at 0.3 miles.

The crest of Copeland Moraine, 700 feet above the trailhead, is gained at 1.2 miles. A sign here marks a junction with a trail originating at Meeker Park. Continuing west, the trail passes a single orange square blaze, stays near the top of the moraine and then moves onto a bench to traverse the side of Lookout Mountain. After descending slightly to Campers Creek, look to the left to find an orange blaze at the creek crossing where the trail is indistinct.

The trail swings south for 200 yards to climb out of Campers Creek. Between here and Hunters Creek the nearly level trail is marked by two orange blazes as it crosses the hummocky terrain. Hunters Creek crossing is marked by a footbridge with a handrail. Beyond here there are widely spaced orange blazes as the trail crosses the bottom and then climbs steeply out of Hunters Creek drainage. The gradient gradually lessens until the near-level trail turns back left to the southwest for 200 yards through seemingly bottomless powder to Sandbeach Lake at 4.2 miles.

ADDITIONAL CONNECTING TRAIL INFORMATION

A trail shown on the USGS topographic map as originating at Meeker Park joins the Sandbeach Lake Trail at 1.2 miles. No access through the private property lining the highway at Meeker Park could be found.

SKILLS RECOMMENDED

Technical skiing
Intermediate. You will probably hike the steep lower section due to lack of snow.

Thereafter the generally moderate slopes on this forest trail are intermediate in difficulty except for a steep section above Hunters Creek at 3.2 miles. With generally excellent snow and little use, there is frequently untracked powder here to make the descent easier.

Endurance

Strenuous. The trip to the lake and return is over eight miles with 2,000 feet altitude gained and lost over a trail that will probably be untracked. If you are alone or in a party where the task of breaking trail falls on only one or two, it can be very strenuous.

Routefinding

Intermediate. In conditions of good visibility it is not difficult to follow this summer hiking trail with widely spaced orange square tree blazes on its route through the forest. Its usage is light however, so you may find it untracked. Look for the orange blaze to the left at the crossing of Campers Creek.

VIEWS

After having caught only infrequent glimpses of its top through the dense trees on the way up, the immense breadth of Mt. Meeker is suddenly revealed to the unsuspecting skier on reaching the clearing at Sandbeach Lake. The rugged profile of Pagoda Mountain is the near skyline to the northwest. Massive Mt. Audubon and the line of other Indian Peaks are visible to the south, beyond the rim of Wild Basin formed by Mt. Copeland, St. Vrain Mountain, and Meadow Mountain.

PRIVATE PROPERTY AND OTHER RESTRICTIONS

Private property at Meeker Park blocks access to the eastern end of a connecting trail shown on the USGS topographic map to join the Sandbeach Lake trail at mile 1.2.

All of the trail except approximately the first half mile is within Rocky Mountain National Park and subject to park regulations. Dogs are not permitted on the trails.

❄ ❄ ❄

TRAIL NO. 2

THUNDER LAKE TRAIL

TRAIL MAPS: 3, 2, 1

SUMMARY

The near-level valley floor west from Copeland Lake is followed for three and a half easy but uninteresting miles into Wild Basin before climbing steeply through switchbacks that are frequently bare or icy to Calypso Cascades and Ouzel Falls. Snow conditions improve dramatically beyond here on this long, generally protected and moderate trail to the source of North St. Vrain Creek. The isolation and grandeur of the snow-plumed peaks and ridge of the continental divide at the head of the valley confirm this is appropriately named Wild Basin.

CLASSIFICATION: Difficult

MAPS (USGS 7.5' quadrangles)

Allens Park (A3)
Isolation Peak (A2)

ELEVATIONS (feet)

Starting....................................8,360
Highest...............................10,760
Cumulative gain 2,400
Cumulative loss..........................120

DISTANCE (miles, one way).......8.2

TIME (hours)

Outbound 4.8
Return 2.7

ACCESS

At Wild Basin Trailhead (A).

Isolation Peak, Eagles Beak from Wild Basin

USAGE

The level of usage is light as far as Ouzel Falls at 4.4 miles and beyond there, very light. The action of the Park Service in moving the trailhead back 0.9 mile to Copeland Lake discourages use of this trail.

SNOW CONDITIONS

Snow conditions are usually poor as far as Ouzel Falls due to the relatively low altitude. The section in the vicinity of Calypso Cascades is frequently icy from freezing of water seeps. Beyond here snow conditions improve steadily with altitude except for a few minor windblown localities to become excellent in the upper reaches.

WIND EXPOSURE

In the initial, low altitude segment of the trail in the valley bottom, the tree cover is widely spaced and interspersed with long clearings so that the effect of the wind is significant. Thereafter the trail is well sheltered by trees with the exception a wind swept corner where the valley and trail turn northwest.

GRADIENT

The gradient for two miles is nearly flat, from there to the crossing of the creek at 3.4 miles, slight. Thereafter the trail climbs steeply through icy switchbacks for 0.3 mile to Calypso Cascades. After a moderate climb to Ouzel Falls, the one mile section to the next crossing of the creek Is nearly flat. The remainder of the trail climbs moderately.

ROUTE DESCRIPTION

From the parking area near Copeland Lake, ski or walk west on the main road up the valley bottom as it crosses the creek to the south side and passes the sign-marked Finch Lake trailhead at 1.8 miles. Continue on the road as it turns left after crossing the creek again and passes through a parking area to the summer trailhead with a large sign at 2.0 miles. A warming hut operated by volunteers from the Enos Mills group of the Colorado Mountain Club in Estes Park is generally open on weekends in the Wild Basin ranger station to the north of here.

The trail continues west along the north side of North St. Vrain Creek to cross the creek on a substantial log footbridge at 3.4 miles. Log steps may be icy on this well-defined section with little altitude gain. The burned area on Meadow Mountain to the south is visible from here. Beyond the bridge, the character of the trail changes abruptly, with steep grades, sharp turns, ice, and protruding rocks and logs on the narrow twisting trail. On the return if poor snow conditions exist, descent of the entire section may be most easily done by walking.

Calypso Cascades is at 3.7 miles. About 200 yards beyond, a burned area is entered. Ouzel Falls with an outhouse, frozen waterfall, and log footbridge is reached at 4.4 miles. A pair of switchbacks at 4.7 miles marks the end of the tedious obstacles. The trail is nearly level past a sign-marked junction with a trail to Ouzel and Bluebird Lakes at 5.2 miles and on to a footbridge crossing of

North St. Vrain Creek at 5.6 miles. There, a steady moderate climb for the remainder of the trail begins.

A switchback at 5.9 miles affords a view of Meadow and St. Vrain Mountains to the southeast and Mt. Copeland to the southwest. The sign-marked junction with a trail to Lion Lakes is reached at 6.4 miles. Orange square tree blazes start at a pair of switchbacks at 6.7 miles and continue for the remainder of the trail. On rounding a windy corner at 6.9 miles a spectacular view of the continental divide from Isolation Peak to Mt. Alice unfolds.

Cross a footbridge at 7.6 miles and head upstream near the drainage to locate the next orange blaze. The blazed trail leads to an outhouse and camping area 200 feet above and north of the patrol cabin before descending to it at the east end of Thunder Lake at 8.2 miles. A shorter unblazed alternate route direct to the lake heads west-northwest from the footbridge at 7.6 miles and climbs only slightly.

ADDITIONAL CONNECTING TRAIL INFORMATION

The sign-marked junction with the summer Finch Lake Trail is at 1.8 miles. The Calypso Cascades Cutoff Trail (2A) junction is at 3.7 miles. This trail connects to the Allens Park-Finch Lake-Pear Reservoir Trail (3).

SKILLS RECOMMENDED

Technical skiing
Advanced. The first three and a half miles to the bridge are easy. The section to Calypso Cascades and Ouzel Falls is moderately difficult in dealing with tedious obstacles and ice on a narrow twisting trail. Beyond here the slopes are moderate and the snow commonly excellent but untracked. There are no particularly difficult sections but you must maintain a low advanced level of skiing over a lengthy trip.

Endurance
Very strenuous. This is a very long day of 16.4 miles round trip and 2,400 feet altitude gained and lost. The lower part of it will probably be on poor snow and the upper on untracked powder.

Routefinding
Intermediate. Only beginner skills are required as far as Ouzel Falls. The trail beyond is almost entirely in trees with most of it blazed with widely spaced orange squares.

VIEWS

Spectacular views are obtained of the peaks at the head of Wild Basin. Mt. Meeker, Longs Peak, and Pagoda Mountain are visible from the burned area at 3.8 miles. Frozen Ouzel Falls at 4.4 miles is of special interest when ice climbers are practicing. A switchback at 5.9 miles affords views to the south across Wild Basin of Meadow and St. Vrain Mountains and Mt. Copeland. As a windy corner at 6.9 miles is rounded a splendid panorama of the continental divide is revealed from Isolation Peak north to Eagles Beak, The Cleaver, Tanima Peak, Boulder-Grand Pass, Pilot Mountain, and Mt. Alice. Close-up views of Boulder-Grand Pass and Chiefs Head Peak are to be had from Thunder Lake.

PRIVATE PROPERTY AND OTHER RESTRICTIONS

All of the trail except approximately the first half mile is in Rocky Mountain Park. Dogs are not permitted on the trails. The patrol cabin at Thunder Lake is not open for public use.

❄ ❄ ❄

TRAIL NO. 2 A

CALYPSO CASCADES CUTOFF TRAIL

TRAIL MAP: 2

SUMMARY

This infrequently skied summer hiking trail is used as a connecting link from lower part of Wild Basin up to the Allens Park-Finch Lake-Pear Reservoir trail. From this junction, one can ski either west to the southern, upper part of Wild Basin on the Allens Park-Finch Lake-Pear Reservoir Trail or east around Meadow Mountain to Allens Park.

CLASSIFICATION: Moderate-difficult

MAPS (USGS 7.5' quadrangle)

Allens Park (A3)

ELEVATIONS (feet)

Starting.....................................9,150
Highest.....................................9,720
Cumulative gain 570
Cumulative loss.............................0

DISTANCE (miles, one way).......1.5

TIME (Hours)

Uphill (east)................................0.7
Downhill (west)...........................0.5

ACCESS

Ski the Thunder Lake Trail (2) west from the Wild Basin Trailhead (A), 3.7 miles to the sign-marked trail junction at Calypso Cascades.

USAGE

Nearly unused. Steep switchbacks discourage its use as ski trail.

SNOW CONDITIONS

Snow conditions here reflect the influence of altitude, ranging from medium at the bottom to good at the top. The narrow trail is sheltered by trees and a north-facing slope from the effects of the wind and sun.

WIND EXPOSURE

The entire trail is protected from the wind by the dense forest.

GRADIENT

The entire trail is steep, gaining 570 feet altitude in a mile and a half with four switchbacks.

ROUTE DESCRIPTION

The orange square blazed trail climbs steadily through four switchbacks from the sign-marked junction at Calypso Cascades eastward up the steep south side of Wild Basin. A sign-marked four-way trail junction is reached at 1.5 miles where the steepness of the slope lessens.

ADDITIONAL CONNECTING TRAIL INFORMATION

The upper or east end of this trail connects with the Allens Park-Finch Lake-Pear Reservoir Trail (3) at mile 1.6. Also at this junction is an unblazed trail to the Finch Lake trailhead near the Wild Basin ranger station.

SKILLS RECOMMENDED

Technical skiing
Intermediate. This is a steep narrow trail with sharp switchbacks to negotiate. Done uphill as part of a loop trip, it is only beginner level.

Endurance
Easy.

Routefinding
Novice. There are no route finding problems on this well-defined trail through dense trees with trail signs at both ends.

VIEWS

Only glimpses of Mt. Meeker are obtained through the trees.

PRIVATE PROPERTY AND OTHER RESTRICTIONS

All of the trail is within Rocky Mountain Park and subject to park regulations. Dogs are not allowed on the trails.

❄ ❄ ❄

TRAIL NO. 3

ALLENS PARK-FINCH LAKE-PEAR RESERVOIR TRAIL

TRAIL MAPS: 3, 2

SUMMARY

A marked change in both snow quality and amount of use is encountered as this trail climbs from the edge of Allens Park village, around the north side of Meadow Mountain to the far reaches of Wild Basin and the edge of the forest near the base of lofty cliffs bounding Mt. Copeland. The low altitude beginning is moderately heavily used and generally has only medium quality snow, whereas the deep powder at the high and isolated far end is ordinarily untracked.

CLASSIFICATION: Difficult

MAPS (USGS 7.5' quadrangles)

Allens Park (A3)
Isolation Peak (A2)

ELEVATIONS (feet)

Starting....................................8900
Highest...................................10600
Cumulative gain 1950
Cumulative loss.........................250

DISTANCE (miles, one way).......5.8

TIME (hours)

Outbound 3.4
Return 2.0

ACCESS

At Allens Park Trailhead (B). Here at a summer parking lot at the edge of Rocky Mountain Park the beginning of the trail is marked with a sign *Allens Park Trail.*

USAGE

Usage varies from moderate at the beginning to very light beyond Finch Lake.

SNOW CONDITIONS

Medium snow conditions characteristic of the relatively low altitude at the beginning improve as altitude is gained to become excellent beyond Finch Lake. Deep untracked powder snow in the trees here can be both a blessing and a curse respectively for the descent and ascent of short steep sections.

WIND EXPOSURE

The entire route is in the protection of trees with the exception of a 500 yard wide burned area midway and the final 600 yards to Pear Reservoir.

GRADIENT

Moderate overall. A short steep section at 1.0 miles where the trail is in the trees gains about 100 feet. Steep sections are also encountered in the deep powder beyond Finch Reservoir and again as the crossing of Pear Creek below Pear Reservoir is approached.

ROUTE DESCRIPTION

The well-defined trail climbs through moderately spaced trees and is marked with orange square tree blazes as it circles to the north side of Meadow Mountain. Pass a junction at 0.7 miles where a trail branches off to the right and continue on to a sign-marked, four way junction at 1.6 miles. Bear left here as directed by signs toward Finch Lake and Pear Reservoir on a trail marked with orange square blazes. Cross a 500 yard wide burned area with standing dead trees and widely-spaced orange square blazes at 2.0 miles. The trail levels off and crosses a drainage on a log footbridge with a handrail at 3.3 miles and then descends a steep 200 feet via four switchbacks to the north end of Finch Lake at 3.8 miles.

The now indistinct trail goes around the north end of the lake and heads southwest staying near the shoreline through a summer camping area and passes the last two orange blazes. Past a sign *Pear Creek,Pear Lake,* it crosses the outlet creek of Finch Lake and then crosses Coney Creek at a log bridge. Although now unblazed and probably untracked, the trail is distinct enough to follow without too much difficulty as it climbs through the large trees, passing to the right of a pond at 4.8 miles and on to a sign marking Pear Creek at 5.4 miles. Here it heads up the left (south) side of the drainage 600 yards to the site of the former rock dam at Pear Reservoir and the base of Mount Copeland (5.8 miles).

ADDITIONAL CONNECTING TRAIL INFORMATION

An unblazed trail at 0.7 miles, usually untracked, goes to the Wild Basin Ranger Station. At the sign-marked, four-way trail junction at 1.6 miles, the first trail to the right or northeast is to Wild Basin Ranger Station and is unblazed. The second trail to the right or west is also to Wild Basin Ranger Station, via the Calypso Cascades Cutoff Trail (2A) and is marked with orange square blazes.
An unmarked junction with the North Gully of St. Vrain Mountain Route (5A) is at the creek crossing 3.3 miles, marked by a log foot bridge with a handrail. This route will almost certainly be untracked.

SPECIFIC SKILLS RECOMMENDED

Technical skiing
Intermediate. Short difficult steep sections are at 1.0 miles and at the switchbacks east of Finch Lake at 3.6 miles. The most difficult part is the steep section beyond Finch Lake which will probably have deep powder.

Endurance
Very strenuous. Twelve miles round trip and 2000 vertical feet are gained and lost. Probably four miles and 700 feet of this will be in untracked deep powder snow. Take some friends to break trail.

Routefinding
Advanced skill is required beyond Finch Lake, novice or beginner skills are adequate for the easily followed trail to there.

VIEWS

Glimpses of Mt. Meeker to the northwest, Twin Sisters to the east, and Mt. Alice to the west are obtained through the trees in the first two miles. At the burned area at 2.0 miles, Chiefs Head, Pagoda Mountain, Longs Peak, and Mt. Meeker are visible four miles to the northwest across Wild Basin.

Finch Lake offers unobstructed views of Mt. Copeland and Elk Tooth. From Pear Reservoir, situated at the base of cliffs soaring up toward Mt. Copeland, Elk Tooth is visible at the head of the valley to the west southwest.

PRIVATE PROPERTY AND OTHER RESTRICTIONS

All of the trail is within Rocky Mountain Park and subject to park regulations. Dogs are not allowed on the trails.

❄ ❄ ❄

TRAIL NO. 4

ROCK CREEK TRAIL

TRAIL MAP: 6

SUMMARY

An easy mile and a half along a wide road following the gentle valley bottom leads to the abandoned Rock Creek ski area. Snow conditions however, may be poor at this low altitude. Beyond the ski area the snow improves steadily with altitude on the north-facing slope as the gradient gradually steepens. The old logging road becomes less obvious and is generally not tracked all the way to the saddle on the east ridge of St. Vrain Mountain.

CLASSIFICATION: Moderate-difficult

MAPS (USGS 7.5' quadrangles)

Allens Park (A3)

ELEVATIONS (feet)

Starting.....................................8580
Highest.................................10680
Cumulative gain 2100

Cumulative loss.............................0

DISTANCE (miles, one way).......3.1

TIME (hours)

Outbound 2.4
Return 1.2

ACCESS

At Rock Creek Trailhead (C).

USAGE

Moderate as far as the old ski area, above there it diminishes from moderate to light and very light near the saddle.

SNOW CONDITIONS

Snow quality improves with distance and altitude along the trail. Below the old ski area it may be very poor due to low altitude, exposure to sunlight, and the effects of vehicles sometimes being driven onto the snowpack. Higher and on a north-facing slope, it improves to medium and good.

WIND EXPOSURE

I haven't experienced much wind here, even in the lower part where the sparse trees offer little protection. The north-south orientation of the valley may diminish the effect of the wind.

GRADIENT

Moderate overall, although the first part to the ski area is nearly flat. Thereafter it increases with altitude until lessening near the saddle at the end.

ROUTE DESCRIPTION

Ski the wide road south, past a sign at 0.3 miles *St. Vrain Mountain Trailhead 1/2 mile,* marking a road which leads west. Continue south on the road along the valley bottom to the old ski area where the valley turns west at 1.4 miles. The wide, easily-recognized trail now climbs steadily and more steeply up the south side of the valley through dense trees with occasional switchbacks. A few dead end logging spurs branch off to the north. If in doubt, take the left branch. The slope lessens and the trail becomes less distinct in the more widely spaced trees as the 10,600 foot saddle on the east ridge of St. Vrain Mountain is approached at 3.1 miles. An alternative to following the road where it becomes indistinct, is to simply head uphill for the ridge on the easy terrain. The ridge may be readily skied east to Point 10,810 by going between rock outcrops on the ridge top.

ADDITIONAL CONNECTING TRAIL INFORMATION

The St. Vrain Mountain Trail (5) branches off at a sign marked junction at 0.3 miles. A cairn-marked junction with the Rock Creek Saddle Route (8B) is at 2.3 miles and 9680 feet. The East Ridge St. Vrain Mountain Route (4A) continues on from the end of the trail.

SPECIFIC SKILLS RECOMMENDED

Technical skiing
If snow conditions aren't prohibitive, the terrain below the ski area is suitable for novice skiers. Above, beginner and eventually intermediate skills are advisable.

Endurance
Moderate, but could be strenuous if a lot of trail has to be broken near the saddle.

Routefinding
Beginner. There are few problems in following this distinct road. Even at the top where the road becomes indistinct, the ridge is nearby and not difficult to find.

VIEWS

The nearby slopes of St. Vrain and Meadow Mountains to the west and northwest block views In those directions. From the ridge line at 3.1 miles, Twin Sisters Peaks are visible to the north northeast while Sawtooth Mountain, Paiute Peak, and Mt. Audubon are visible to the southwest across the valley of Middle St. Vrain Creek. The bench route followed by the Coney Flats Trail (10) from Beaver Reservoir to Coney Flats is visible across the valley to the south.

PRIVATE PROPERTY AND OTHER RESTRICTIONS

None.

❄ ❄ ❄

TRAIL NO. 4A

EAST RIDGE ST. VRAIN MOUNTAIN ROUTE

TRAIL MAP: 5

SUMMARY

This unmarked and almost certainly untracked route climbs above timberline on the exposed eastern slopes of St. Vrain Mountain to connect the Rock Creek Trail (4) with the St. Vrain Mountain Trail (5) and the North Gully St. Vrain Mountain Route (5A). Loop trips around the head of Rock Creek and around Meadow Mountain can be done with this route as the high link.

CLASSIFICATION: Difficult

MAPS (USGS 7.5' quadrangles)

Allens Park (A3)

ELEVATIONS (feet)

Starting...................................10680
Highest....................................11330
Cumulative gain 650
Cumulative loss..........................130

DISTANCE (miles, one way).......1.5

TIME (hours)

Outbound 1.2
Return 0.8

ACCESS

From the Rock Creek Trailhead (C), ski 3.1 miles to the end of the Rock Creek Trail (4).

USAGE

Nearly unused.

SNOW CONDITIONS

Snow conditions on this untracked route are good to excellent in the shelter of the trees at the start but deteriorate to poor or very poor above timberline due to the effect of the wind. Expect wind slab, sastrugi, and bare tundra.

WIND EXPOSURE

Very severe as most of the route is above timberline.

GRADIENT

A constant steep gradient is encountered until timberline is reached at 11,200 ft. Thereafter the gradient is nearly flat.

ROUTE DESCRIPTION

From the end of the Rock Creek Trail (4), head west up the ridge through widely spaced trees on a climb of 600 feet. Follow the ridge to the northwest above timberline and traverse across the eastern slopes of St. Vrain Mountain to the saddle between it and Peak 11,478. Continue the traverse onto the western slopes of Peak 11,478 and on to the saddle between it and Meadow Mountain at 1.5 miles.

ADDITIONAL CONNECTING TRAIL INFORMATION

An unmarked junction with both the North Gully St. Vrain Mountain Route (5A) and the St. Vrain Mountain Trail (5) is at the saddle at the end of the route.

SPECIFIC SKILLS RECOMMENDED

Technical skiing
Advanced. The difficulties are more with snow conditions rather than terrain.

Endurance
Very strenuous, particularly in breaking trail up the ridge.

Routefinding
Advanced routefinding skills are necessary to make any of the loop trips of which this route is part.

VIEWS

In addition to the views to the north northeast of Twin Sisters Peaks and to the southwest of Sawtooth Peak, Paiute Peak, and Mt. Audubon which were obtained lower from the Rock Creek Trail, views to the west and north are now open without being blocked by Meadow Mountain. The view across Wild Basin includes Elk Tooth, Ogalalla Peak, Mt. Copeland, Isolation Peak, Mt. Alice, Chiefs Head Peak, Pagoda Mountain, Longs Peak, and Mt. Meeker.

PRIVATE PROPERTY AND OTHER RESTRICTIONS

None.

❅ ❅ ❅

TRAIL NO. 5

ST. VRAIN MOUNTAIN TRAIL

TRAIL MAPS: 6, 5

SUMMARY

This trail climbs a vigorous 2600 feet in 3.5 miles to a high saddle between Meadow Mountain and St. Vrain Mountain. There one can continue another 900 feet to the summit of St. Vrain Mountain or 400 feet to the top of Meadow Mountain. Descent from the saddle can be by either the East Ridge St. Vrain Mountain Trail (4A) or North Gully St. Vrain Mountain Route (5A) to give challenging loop trips. The high saddle is an superb vantage point for views across Wild Basin of peaks on the continental divide.

CLASSIFICATION: Difficult

MAPS (USGS 7.5' quadrangles)

Allens Park (A3)

ELEVATIONS (feet)

Starting.....................................8580
Highest 11200

Cumulative gain 2620
Cumulative loss.............................0

DISTANCE (miles, one way).......3.5

TIME (hours)

Outbound 3.0
Return 1.4

ACCESS

From Rock Creek Trailhead (C), ski 0.3 miles south on the Rock Creek Trail (4) to a sign-marked junction.

USAGE

Very light.

SNOW CONDITIONS

Poor to medium conditions can be expected at the bottom, improving to medium to good as one gains altitude but deteriorating to poor above timberline.

WIND EXPOSURE

Very exposed, especially at the above-timberline saddle and in the open bowl on the ascent. The trees are too small and widely spaced to offer much shelter.

GRADIENT

Unremittingly steep for nearly the entire route.

ROUTE DESCRIPTION

From the junction at 0.3 miles on the Rock Creek Trail (4), head west on the road identified with the sign *St. Vrain Mountain Trailhead 1/2 mile,* as it climbs on a curving route to a sign-marked summer trailhead and end of the road at 0.5 miles. From here the unblazed but distinct trail climbs steadily through aspen and evergreen trees and angles into the tributary drainage to Rock Creek as an open treeless bowl comes into view ahead. The summer trail stays to the right of the drainage with several switchbacks, but the snow may be better in the drainage. Switchback to the left at 10,200 feet and climb 500 yards through scattered trees, then switchback right to cross above the steepest part of the bowl. Proceed up the right side of the now less steep drainage through scattered low trees to the 10,200 foot saddle between Meadow Mountain and Peak 11,478 and end of the route at 3.5 miles.

ADDITIONAL CONNECTING TRAILS INFORMATION

Unmarked junctions with the North Gully St. Vrain Mountain Route (5A) and East Ridge St. Vrain Mountain Route (4A) are at the 10,200 saddle.

SPECIFIC SKILLS RECOMMENDED

Technical skiing
Advanced skills are required to descend the 2600 feet of steep terrain.

Endurance
Strenuous, for both climbing and descending 2600 feet.

Routefinding
Intermediate. You probably won't find this route tracked and it may be difficult to stay on the summer trail, but the terrain is simple.

VIEWS

From the west side of the saddle, one has a spectacular vista (left to right) across Wild Basin to Elk Tooth, Ogallala Peak, Copeland Mountain, Isolation Peak, Tanima Peak, Mt. Alice, Chiefs Head Peak, Pagoda Mountain, Longs Peak, and Mt. Meeker.

PRIVATE PROPERTY AND OTHER RESTRICTIONS

None

❄ ❄ ❄

TRAIL NO. 5 A

NORTH GULLY ST.VRAIN MOUNTAIN ROUTE

TRAIL MAP: 5

SUMMARY

This off-trail route descends 1100 feet down a steep drainage from the saddle between Meadow and St. Vrain Mountains into Wild Basin. When linked with the Allens Park-Finch Lake-Pear Reservoir Trail and the St. Vrain Mountain Trail, it forms a circular route from Allens Park around Meadow Mountain. It is not recommended for uphill travel.

CLASSIFICATION: Very difficult.

MAPS (USGS 7.5' quadrangles)

Allens Park (A3)

ELEVATIONS (feet)

Starting 11200
Highest 11200
Cumulative gain 0
Cumulative loss 1100

DISTANCE (miles, one way) 1.3

TIME (hours)

Outbound (down) 0.7
Return (up) 2.0

ACCESS

From Rock Creek Trailhead (C), ski the Rock Creek Trail (4) and then the East Ridge St. Vrain Mountain Route (4A) to the 11,200 foot saddle where this trail begins, a total distance of 4.6 miles.

Alternatively, the St. Vrain Mountain Trail (5) provides a 3.8 mile access to the saddle.

USAGE

Nearly unused.

SNOW CONDITIONS

High altitude, a north-facing slope, and protection by trees all combine to make excellent snow for a descent but exhausting deep snow for climbing.

WIND EXPOSURE

None except at the above-timberline start of the route.

GRADIENT

Overall very steep, moderate at the top and nearly flat at the bottom.

ROUTE DESCRIPTION

From the 11,200 foot saddle between Meadow Mountain and Peak 11,478, head west northwest to enter the drainage on a gentle slope through widely spaced trees. As the trees become more closely spaced, the slope steepens and one is forced into the gully by steep side slopes. Both the side slopes and the general stream gradient flatten before the end of the route is reached at a junction with the Allens Park-Finch Lake-Pear Reservoir Trail (3) at 10,100 feet altitude and 1.3 miles. Aids to recognizing this trail (3) if it is untracked, are widely spaced orange square trail blazes and a log footbridge with a handrail where it crosses one of several stream channels in the vicinity of the junction.

ADDITIONAL CONNECTING TRAILS INFORMATION

Unmarked junctions with the East Ridge St. Vrain Mountain Route (4A) and the St. Vrain Mountain Trail (5) are at the 11,200 foot saddle at the beginning of the route. An unmarked junction with the Allens Park-Finch Lake-Pear Reservoir Trail (3) is at the north end of the route.

SPECIFIC SKILLS RECOMMENDED

Technical skiing
Expert skills are required to descend the steep gully with dense trees and deep powder snow.

Endurance
Very strenuous. This route has to be linked with other routes that give access to it. It would be extraordinarily strenuous to ascend the untracked deep powder snow 1100 feet up this steep gradient.

Routefinding
Advanced skills are required to link this route with the routes that give access and egress. At the north end, one can easily fail to recognize the Allens Park-Pear Reservoir Trail if it is untracked. An altimeter is helpful here.

VIEWS

None other than at the start. These are listed in the trail descriptions for the connecting routes, the St. Vrain Mountain Trail (5) and the East Ridge St. Vrain Mountain Route (4A).

PRIVATE PROPERTY AND OTHER RESTRICTIONS

Part of the trail is within Rocky Mountain Park, dogs are not permitted.

❄ ❄ ❄

TRAIL NO. 6

MIDDLE ST. VRAIN ROAD

TRAIL MAPS: 6, 5

SUMMARY

Although used by snowmobilers, this pleasant road up the valley bottom of the Middle St. Vrain Creek provides easy access to the boundary of the Indian Peaks Wilderness from the Peak to Peak highway at Peaceful Valley, a distance of nearly five miles. It parallels the Buchanan Pass Trail (7) and may have better snow. It is the easy and faster route to ski downhill.

CLASSIFICATION: Moderate

MAPS (USGS 7.5' quadrangles)

Allens Park (A3)

ELEVATIONS (feet)

Starting.....................................8520
Highest.....................................9600
Cumulative gain 1080

Cumulative loss.............................0

DISTANCE (miles, one way).......4.7

TIME (hours)

Outbound 2.0
Return 1.5

ACCESS

At Peaceful Valley Trailhead (D).

Sawtooth Mountain

USAGE

Moderate at beginning, light at far end.

SNOW CONDITIONS

Poor at beginning, improving to good to excellent at far end. Except for the first mile, the road stays near the shaded south side of the valley. The snowmobile traffic may help the snow conditions in the lower section by providing a packed base.

WIND EXPOSURE

Slight, the road is generally in trees but there are a few clearings in the lower part where this protection is lacking.

GRADIENT

Although the overall gradient is slight and there are no steep sections, the route gains 1080 feet in the 4.7 miles.

ROUTE DESCRIPTION

Ski west on the road up the valley bottom, passing a trail sign for the Buchanan Pass Trail (7) in 200 yards at a vehicle bridge where the road crosses to the north side of the valley. At 0.8 miles the road crosses back over the creek to pass through the Camp Dick summer campground. From here the road climbs steadily up the south side of the straight valley. At 2.6 miles a four post barrier to vehicular crossing of the creek can be seen at the side of the road. Pass a sign marked junction where the Coney Flats-Middle St. Vrain Trail (10B) descends into the valley at 4.6 miles and continue on another 220 yards to the end of the road at a footbridge with a handrail and the sign-marked wilderness boundary at 4.7 miles.

ADDITIONAL CONNECTING TRAILS INFORMATION

The Buchanan Pass Trail (7) branches off at a sign-marked junction at a vehicle bridge at 200 yards. At 0.3 miles the Park Creek Trail (8), turns back sharply and uphill at a sign *Bunce School Road*. The Buchanan Pass Trail crosses the road at a sign-marked junction at 1.1 miles and continues to parallel it. The Buchanan Pass Trail can be easily reached at the four post barrier at 2.6 miles where it is only 100 yards to the north across a clearing.

The junction with the Coney Flats-Middle St. Vrain Trail (10B) is at 4.6 miles at a sign-marked junction and yet another junction with the paralleling Buchanan Pass Trail is at the end of the route at 4.7 miles and across the foot bridge.

SPECIFIC SKILLS RECOMMENDED

Technical skiing
Novice at beginning, beginner if extended to the upper part.

Endurance
Moderate if the entire route is done.

Routefinding
Novice.

VIEWS

Sawtooth Mountain and Buchanan Pass to its right are visible at the head of the valley throughout most of the trip. Ogalalla Peak and Elk Tooth appear as the valley turns northwest.

PRIVATE PROPERTY AND OTHER RESTRICTIONS

None.

❄ ❄ ❄

TRAIL NO. 7

BUCHANAN PASS TRAIL

TRAIL MAPS: 6, 5

SUMMARY

The straight, steadily rising valley floor of the Middle St. Vrain is followed west on a lengthy tour from the Peaceful Valley Trailhead, 4.8 miles to the Indian Peaks Wilderness boundary and a junction with the parallel Middle St. Vrain Road. The trail then turns to the northwest and continues up the valley another mile and a half to link with the St. Vrain Glacier Trail.

CLASSIFICATION: Moderate-difficult

MAPS (USGS 7.5' quadrangles)

Allens Park (A3)

ELEVATIONS (feet)

Starting......................................8520
Highest.....................................9910
Cumulative gain 1390
Cumulative loss............................0

DISTANCE (miles, one way).......6.3

TIME (hours)

Outbound 3.4
Return 2.7

ACCESS

From Peaceful Valley Trailhead (D), ski west 200 yards on the Middle St. Vrain Road (6) to the sign-marked trail junction at a vehicle bridge.

USAGE

Light at the beginning, decreasing to very light at the upper end.

SNOW CONDITIONS

Poor at the beginning due to the low altitude and exposure to sunlight on the north side of the valley but improving to good at the upper end. The section where the valley turns northwest is usually poor.

WIND EXPOSURE

The treeless section near the wilderness boundary where the valley turns northwest is extremely windy.

Elktooth Mountain from Middle St. Vrain Valley

GRADIENT

The gradient is slight but steady, gaining 1400 feet in 6.8 miles.

ROUTE DESCRIPTION

From the start at the vehicle bridge, the blue diamond blazed trail heads up the south side of the valley through dense trees. A sign-marked junction with the North Sourdough Trail (9) is passed at 0.7 miles. At 1.2 miles the trail crosses the Middle St. Vrain Road (6) and the creek on a footbridge to the northern side of the valley. Further on, a short climb leads to the sign-marked Timberline Falls on a rocky ledge at 3.1 miles.

Stay on the right side of the valley on entering a wind-swept treeless area near the turn of the valley. Continue past a distinctive slender 15 foot high gneissic boulder 340 yards to a blue diamond blaze on a post. Turn left and cross the valley bottom 50 yards to a junction at 4.8 miles with the Middle St. Vrain Road (6) at a footbridge on the creek.

Continue up the broad open valley on the unblazed jeep road. The road enters the shelter of trees near signs marking the Red Deer Cutoff and St. Vrain Mountain summer trails and the wilderness boundary at 5.4 miles. After passing through an area of dead trees, a sign-marked junction is reached at 6.3 miles. The summer Buchanan Pass Trail crosses the creek on a footbridge with a handrail to switchback and climb south on the side of the valley toward the pass. The St. Vrain Glacier Trail (7A) continues up the valley and the Buchanan Pass Trail as described here, ends.

45

ADDITIONAL CONNECTING TRAILS INFORMATION

A sign-marked junction with the North Sourdough Trail (9) is at 0.7 miles. The parallel Middle St. Vrain Road (6) is crossed at 1.1 miles and a junction at its far end is reached at 4.8 miles. The St. Vrain Glacier Trail (7A) starts at the end of this trail at 6.3 miles.

SPECIFIC SKILLS RECOMMENDED

Technical skiing
Beginner. The tight turns and narrowness of this summer hiking trail are bothersome.

Endurance
Moderate. Its all very easy skiing but lengthy.

Routefinding
Beginner. The only problem might be in finding the junction with the Middle St. Vrain Road at 4.8 miles. Visibility here is frequently restricted by blowing snow.

VIEWS

Sawtooth Mountain and Paiute Peak come into view near the turn in the valley. Elk Tooth and Ogalalla Peak come into view at the head of the valley after the turn.

PRIVATE PROPERTY AND OTHER RESTRICTIONS

Beyond the turn of the valley at 4.8 miles, the trail is within the Indian Peaks Wilderness.

❄ ❄ ❄

TRAIL NO. 7A

ST. VRAIN GLACIER TRAIL

TRAIL MAPS: 5, 4

SUMMARY

The head of this secluded valley in the Indian Peaks Wilderness is nestled beneath the rock buttresses and snow couloirs of Elk Tooth. Reached by an off-trail and little used route over easy terrain up the Middle St. Vrain valley from the end of the Buchanan Pass Trail, it lies a total of nine and a half miles from the Peaceful Valley Trailhead.

CLASSIFICATION: Difficult

MAPS (USGS 7.5' quadrangles)

Allens Park (A3)
Isolation Peak (A2)

ELEVATIONS (feet)

```
Starting....................................9910
Highest...................................10900
Cumulative gain .........................990
Cumulative loss.............................0
```

DISTANCE (miles, one way).......2.4

TIME (hours)

```
Outbound ...................................2.4
Return .........................................1.2
```

ACCESS

From Beaver Reservoir North Trailhead (E), ski 3.2 miles to the end of the Coney Flats Trail (10) at Coney Flats. Drop 0.6 mile into the valley on the Coney Flats-Middle St. Vrain Trail (10B) to a junction with the Middle St. Vrain Road (6). Follow this road west 0.1 mile to a junction with the Buchanan Pass Trail (7) which is followed 1.5 miles to its end. A total distance of 5.4 miles. Even with the 230 foot descent from Coney Flats into the valley, this route is 0.9 mile shorter and saves 220 feet of climbing compared to the access routes from Peaceful Valley described below.

From Peaceful Valley Trailhead (D), ski 6.3 miles to the end of the Buchanan Pass Trail (7). The parallel Middle St. Vrain Road (6) is faster and may be substituted for the initial 4.8 miles.

USAGE

Nearly unused.

SNOW CONDITIONS

Excellent, but expect to break trail.

WIND EXPOSURE

Low. The route is generally among widely space tall trees. Only on the road near the beginning and on the upper part where the valley floor climbs above timberline is the route exposed.

GRADIENT

Slight.

ROUTE DESCRIPTION

Continue up the bottom of the valley following the jeep road to where it turns left to cross the creek at 0.7 miles. Pick a route on the easy terrain through the widely spaced tall trees along the right side of the valley floor. Pass a boulder field at 1.1 miles and continue to the above timberline lake at the base of Elk Tooth, 2.7 miles and 10,900 feet.

ADDITIONAL CONNECTING TRAIL INFORMATION

The trail begins at the end of the Buchanan Pass Trail (7) as described here. Here the summer Buchanan Pass Trail turns left to cross a footbridge and climb back up the side of the valley.

Surveying the St. Vrain glaciers

SPECIFIC SKILLS RECOMMENDED

Technical skiing
Only beginner skills are necessary.

Endurance
Very strenuous due to the long access and the high probability of breaking trail.

Routefinding
Advanced, the off-trail route follows the valley bottom but it is nearly unused and remote.

VIEWS

Elk Tooth is visible near the head of the valley throughout the trip. From the upper part of the route, Ogallala Peak is at the head of the valley while the St. Vrain Glaciers descend from cirques along the continental divide on the left.

PRIVATE PROPERTY AND OTHER RESTRICTIONS

The entire route is within the Indian Peaks Wilderness.

❄ ❄ ❄

TRAIL NO. 8

PARK CREEK TRAIL

TRAIL MAP: 6

SUMMARY

This pleasant infrequently-traveled forest trail offers good snow at a relatively low altitude. In sequence with the Rock Creek Saddle Trail, it is the only route connecting the northern trails in the Rock Creek drainage and Wild Basin with those of the Middle St. Vrain valley.

CLASSIFICATION: Moderate-difficult.

MAPS (USGS 7.5' quadrangles)

Allens Park (A3)

ELEVATIONS (feet)

Starting.....................................8560
Highest.....................................9760
Cumulative gain 1200
Cumulative loss............................0

DISTANCE (miles, one way).......3.3

TIME (hours)

Outbound 2.7
Return 1.4

ACCESS

From Peaceful Valley Trailhead (D), ski west 0.3 miles on the Middle St. Vrain Road (6) to the sign *Bunce School Road*.

USAGE

Nearly unused.

SNOW CONDITIONS

Medium overall. Starting snow conditions are very poor on the south facing slope, but improve greatly at Park Creek.

WIND EXPOSURE

None except at the beginning.

GRADIENT

Slight overall, with a moderate gradient at the end.

ROUTE DESCRIPTION

From the turn-off on the Middle St. Vrain Road (6), climb north through two switchbacks 200 feet onto a bench. Turn left at 1.0 miles off the main road onto a jeep road. This is 70 yards past the second slight rise after reaching the bench and is 340 yards past the second switchback.

Follow this jeep road north as it crosses to the north side of Park Creek and then follows the creek west past a rock quarry at 1.5 miles. At 1.7 miles take the left fork, cross Park Creek, and follow the well-defined trail upstream. At a 100 yard diameter clearing at 2.1 miles, the trail turns right, traverses, climbs toward the rocky outcrop of Peak 10,583 and makes another right turn in a 70 yard clearing. Switchback to the left after 200 yards onto a climbing traverse to the northwest.

Turn right at a five foot tall red-brown stump at 2.8 miles and 9,360 feet altitude. Switchback left in 100 yards onto a 500 yard near-level traverse, then switchback right 100 yards to where the trail turns uphill and ends at 3.3 miles and 9,760 feet altitude.
The Rock Creek Saddle Route (8B) continues on from the end of this trail.

ADDITIONAL CONNECTING TRAIL INFORMATION

The Logging Road Spur (8A) branches off at the rock quarry at 1.5 miles.

SPECIFIC SKILLS RECOMMENDED

Technical skiing
Beginner.

Endurance
Moderate, but expect to break trail.

Routefinding
Advanced, the route description is complex.

VIEWS

Mt. Audubon and Sawtooth Mountain are visible to the west from the upper part of the trail.

PRIVATE PROPERTY AND OTHER RESTRICTIONS

None.

❄ ❄ ❄

TRAIL NO. 8A

LOGGING ROAD SPUR

TRAIL MAP: 6

SUMMARY

This short, infrequently traveled, low altitude, sheltered trail through the trees near Peaceful Valley is an interesting addition to the overcrowded easy trails of the area. Its a good trail for the inexperienced skier to gain experience in breaking trail and routefinding when snow conditions are good.

CLASSIFICATION: Moderate.

MAPS (USGS 7.5' quadrangles)

Allens Park (A3)

ELEVATIONS (feet)

Starting.....................................8870
Highest......................................9220
Cumulative gain 350
Cumulative loss..............................0

DISTANCE (miles, one way).......1.0

TIME (hours)

Outbound 0.7
Return 0.4

ACCESS

From Peaceful Valley Trailhead (D), ski west up the valley 0.3 miles on the Middle St. Vrain Road (6), then north out of the valley 1.5 miles on the Park Creek Trail (8). A total distance of 1.8 miles.

USAGE

Nearly unused.

SNOW CONDITIONS

Generally poor due to the low altitude, but definitely better than that encountered on the Park Creek Trail switchbacks used to gain access. The best snow is on the lower part.

WIND EXPOSURE

The lower part is well sheltered by trees, the upper is less so.

GRADIENT

Generally slight, increasing to moderate at the upper end.

ROUTE DESCRIPTION

From the junction at the rock quarry at 1.5 miles on the Park Creek Trail (8), ski south on a jeep road which winds among the large trees found in the area before heading uphill to end at 1.0 miles in a wind-swept clearing cluttered with logging cable.

ADDITIONAL CONNECTING TRAIL INFORMATION

None.

SPECIFIC SKILLS RECOMMENDED

Technical skiing
Beginner.

Endurance
Very easy.

Routefinding
Beginner.

VIEWS

None.

PRIVATE PROPERTY AND OTHER RESTRICTIONS

None.

❄ ❄ ❄

TRAIL NO. 8B

ROCK CREEK SADDLE ROUTE

TRAIL MAP: 6

SUMMARY

An off-trail route through a 10,100 foot saddle that, in conjunction with the Park Creek Trail, connects the trails in Rock Creek and Wild Basin with those in the Middle St. Vrain valley and south.

CLASSIFICATION: Difficult.

MAPS (USGS 7.5' quadrangles)

Allens Park (A3)

ELEVATIONS (feet)

Starting..................................9760
Highest..................................10140
Cumulative gain 380
Cumulative loss..........................420

DISTANCE (miles, one way).......1.8

TIME (hours)

Outbound (southbound) 1.5
Return (northbound)....................1.5

ACCESS

South end. From Peaceful Valley Trailhead (D), ski 0.3 mile on the Middle St. Vrain Road (6), then 3.3 miles to the end of the Park Creek Trail (8). A total distance of 3.6 miles.

North end. From the Rock Creek Trailhead (C), ski the Rock Creek Trail (4) 2.3 miles to a cairn-marked junction at 9680 feet.

USAGE

Nearly unused.

SNOW CONDITIONS

Expect medium snow quality for the southernmost section on the climb toward the saddle. Snow quality where the route traverses the steep side slope leading into the saddle is very poor and may require walking. Snow quality on the tree sheltered north facing slope north of the saddle is good.

WIND EXPOSURE

Some minor exposure south of the saddle, but generally well protected by trees.

GRADIENT

Moderate on the south side. The north side is moderate but has two steep sections.

ROUTE DESCRIPTION

From the end of the Park Creek Trail (8), proceed on a moderate climbing traverse to the west on easy terrain through widely spaced trees. As the slope lessens, bear more to the right (north) to pass through the gentle saddle at 0.6 miles with a low rock outcrop on your right. This is the saddle between Park Creek and the unnamed tributary to Middle St. Vrain Creek to the west.

Continue on a level traverse to the north across a steep west-facing slope with poor snow and exposed logs and boulders to the saddle between Middle St.

Vrain and Rock Creek at 0.9 miles. Follow a faint flagged trail northwest to a junction with the RoCreek Trail (4) at 1.8 miles. The generally gently descending traverse contains two steep sections.

ADDITIONAL CONNECTING TRAIL INFORMATION

None.

SPECIFIC SKILLS RECOMMENDED

Technical skiing
Advanced skill is required to handle the short steep descents on untracked snow through thick trees.

Endurance
Moderate.

Routefinding
Advanced routefinding skills are necessary to follow the southern part of the route to the two saddles. The route north from the saddle is flagged.

VIEWS

Mt. Audubon, Sawtooth Mountain, and Buchanan Pass are visible to the west from the start of the route to the pass. Longs Peak and Mt. Meeker come into view to the north through the pass.

PRIVATE PROPERTY AND OTHER RESTRICTIONS

None.

❄ ❄ ❄

TRAIL NO. 9

NORTH SOURDOUGH TRAIL

TRAIL MAPS: 6, 8

SUMMARY

The northernmost of three segments of the Sourdough Trail, it climbs steeply out of the Middle St. Vrain Valley on a switchbacked course through dense trees to connect the Peaceful Valley Trailhead and Middle St. Vrain valley with Beaver Reservoir.

CLASSIFICATION: Moderate-difficult

MAPS (USGS 7.5' quadrangles)

Allens Park (A3)
Ward (B3)

ELEVATIONS (feet)

Starting.....................................8600
Highest......................................9160
Cumulative gain 540
Cumulative loss.............................0

DISTANCE (miles, one way).......1.6

TIME (hours)

Outbound (southbound) 1.3
Return (northbound)....................1.0

ACCESS

North end. From Peaceful Valley Trailhead (D), ski 0.1 mile west on the Middle St. Vrain Road (6), then 0.7 miles on the Buchanan Pass Trail (7). A total distance of 0.8 miles.

South end. At Beaver Reservoir East Trailhead (F).

USAGE

Very light.

SNOW CONDITIONS

Medium conditions are determined by a north facing slope and dense trees but at a relatively low altitude.

WIND EXPOSURE

None, protected by trees.

GRADIENT

The climb out of the valley is initially steep, gaining 300 feet in 0.4 mile, but moderate thereafter.

ROUTE DESCRIPTION

From a junction at 0.7 mile on the Buchanan Pass Trail (7), marked with a sign *Beaver Reservoir,* the unblazed trail climbs up the south side of the Middle St. Vrain valley through four switchbacks as it crosses and recrosses a steep gully. Pass an sign-marked junction to the right at 0.4 miles and traverse to the left (east) to an overlook point.

The trail now climbs more gradually to the south. Keep to the left at junctions with two alternate trails, cross Beaver Creek at 1.1 miles, and contour to the east around a low rounded hill. Pass under a telephone line at 1.5 miles and continue to the junction with the Beaver Reservoir road at 1.6 miles.

ADDITIONAL CONNECTING TRAILS INFORMATION

An unmarked junction with the Beaver Reservoir Cutoff Trail (9A) is at 0.4 miles.

The Middle Sourdough Trail (12) continues to the south from the end of this trail.

SPECIFIC SKILLS RECOMMENDED

Technical skiing
Intermediate skill for southbound or uphill travel, advanced for downhill.

Endurance
Easy.

Routefinding
Beginner, the route is blue diamond blazed but may be untracked. It is generally an easy to follow, distinct trail through trees.

VIEWS

Good views of Mt. Audubon and Sawtooth Mountain are to be had from anywhere in the vicinity of Beaver Reservoir. From the overlook at 0.4 miles, Elk Tooth is seen at the head of the valley and St. Vrain Mountain and Meadow Mountain to the north across the valley.

PRIVATE PROPERTY AND OTHER RESTRICTIONS

None.

❄ ❄ ❄

TRAIL NO. 9A

BEAVER RESERVOIR CUTOFF TRAIL

TRAIL MAP: 8

SUMMARY

An easy short trail through the woods east of Beaver Reservoir, it connects the North Sourdough Trail with the Beaver Reservoir North Trailhead. With this as a connecting link, loop trips from Peaceful Valley Trailhead to Coney Flats are possible. One can ski west to Coney Flats on the Coney Flats Trail and return by the Middle St. Vrain Road or Buchanan Pass Trail.

CLASSIFICATION: Moderate.

MAPS (USGS 7.5' quadrangles)

Allens Park (A3)
Ward (B3)

ELEVATIONS (feet)

```
Starting....................................9190
Highest.....................................9190
Cumulative gain ...........................0
Cumulative loss........................270
```

DISTANCE (miles, one way).......0.8

TIME (hours)

```
Outbound (northeast)..................0.4
Return (southwest)......................0.6
```

ACCESS

At Beaver Reservoir North Trailhead (E).

USAGE

Nearly unused.

SNOW CONDITIONS

Medium.

WIND EXPOSURE

Very little.

GRADIENT

Slight.

ROUTE DESCRIPTION

From the Beaver Reservoir North Trailhead (E), ski 50 yards north on the Coney Flats Trail (10). Turn right at a sign, *Beaver Reservoir Trail* onto the blue diamond blazed trail. Turn right again at forks at 170 and 360 yards. The trail descends past a pond on the right to the sign-marked junction with the North Sourdough Trail (9) at 0.8 miles.

ADDITIONAL CONNECTING TRAIL INFORMATION

None.

SPECIFIC SKILLS RECOMMENDED

Technical skiing
Beginner.

Endurance
Very easy.

Routefinding

Beginner, the trail may not be tracked.

VIEWS

None.

PRIVATE PROPERTY AND OTHER RESTRICTIONS

None.

❀ ❀ ❀

TRAIL NO. 10

CONEY FLATS TRAIL

TRAIL MAPS: 8, 6, 5

SUMMARY

This popular trail follows a jeep road west from Beaver Reservoir over a forested peneplain terrain. The moderate but lengthy climb to the Indian Peaks Wilderness boundary ends at wind-swept Coney Flats.

CLASSIFICATION: Moderate.

MAPS (USGS 7.5' quadrangles)

Allens Park (A3)
Ward (B3)

ELEVATIONS (feet)

Starting.....................................9190
Highest.....................................9790
Cumulative gain 600
Cumulative loss.............................0

DISTANCE (miles, one way).......3.2

TIME (hours)

Outbound 1.9
Return 1.3

ACCESS

At Beaver Reservoir North Trailhead (E).

USAGE

Moderate.

SNOW CONDITIONS

Medium.

WIND EXPOSURE

Medium forest cover generally provides adequate protection from the wind. The last 400 yards are however, fully exposed to the frequent, strong westerly gales.

GRADIENT

Slight.

ROUTE DESCRIPTION

From the Beaver Reservoir Trailhead (E), ski the easily followed jeep road west. Take the right fork at a junction at 1.3 miles marked with a sign directing vehicles left and skiers right. Pass through private property marked with a sign and three cabins at 1.7 miles. At 2.6 miles, again stay right at a sign directing vehicles left and skiers right. Stay to the right of steeper slopes as the trail becomes more difficult to follow where it enters an area of stunted trees and drifts. Pass a large sign *Coney 4WD Route* at 3.0 miles and continue west 270 yards more to the Indian Peaks Wilderness boundary and a sign *Coney Flats Trailhead* at 3.2 miles.

ADDITIONAL CONNECTING TRAIL INFORMATION

Junctions with the alternate loop of the Four Wheel Drive Trail (10) are at 1.3 and 2.6 miles.

SPECIFIC SKILLS RECOMMENDED

Technical skiing
Beginner.

Endurance
Moderate.

Routefinding
Beginner. The wide jeep road is easy to follow until an area of stunted trees and drifted snow is reached at about three miles.

VIEWS

The massive bulk of Mt. Audubon is to the southwest. Sawtooth Mountain, Buchanan Pass, and Elk Tooth are in view at the head of the valley to the west. St. Vrain Mountain is across the valley to the northwest.

PRIVATE PROPERTY AND OTHER RESTRICTIONS

Stay on the trail where it passes through private property at 1.7 miles.

❄ ❄ ❄

TRAIL NO. 10A

FOUR WHEEL DRIVE TRAIL

TRAIL MAPS: 6, 8, 7, 5

SUMMARY

An alternate to the Coney Flats Trail, it allows one to make a solitary, below-timberline loop near Coney Flats. In addition, it provides access to the Firebreak Cutoff Route and a shortcut to the north end of the Beaver Creek Route.

CLASSIFICATION: Moderate-difficult.

MAPS (USGS 7.5' quadrangles)

Allens Park (A3)
Ward (B3)

ELEVATIONS (feet)

Starting....................................9590
Highest....................................9880
Cumulative gain 600
Cumulative loss............................0

DISTANCE (miles, one way).......1.8

TIME (hours)

Outbound 1.2
Return 0.9

ACCESS

East end. From Beaver Reservoir North Trailhead (E), ski 1.3 miles west on the Coney Flats Trail (10).

West end. From Beaver Reservoir North Trailhead (E), ski 2.6 miles west on the Coney Flats Trail.

USAGE

Nearly unused.

SNOW CONDITIONS

Good. You will probably break trail.

WIND EXPOSURE

The trail is well sheltered by trees from the wind.

GRADIENT

Moderate.

ROUTE DESCRIPTION

At 1.3 miles on the Coney Flats Trail (10), take the left fork at a sign directing vehicles and motorbikes left and hikers and skiers right. This junction is 500 yards east of the private cabins at mile 1.7 on the Coney Flats Trail.

At 0.4 miles the easily followed jeep road switchbacks right as the second and larger of two ponds is passed on your left, and becomes less distinct as it climbs to the west. At 1.3 miles and 9850 feet altitude, take the right fork onto a near level route which then descends to a junction with the Coney Flats Trail (10) at 1.8 miles.

ADDITIONAL CONNECTING TRAIL INFORMATION

An unmarked junction with the Firebreak Cutoff Trail (21B) is at the switchback at 0.4 miles.

The junction at 1.8 miles is 0.6 miles east of the lake at Coney Flats. It is marked with a sign directing hikers to the lower Coney Flats Trail and vehicles to the higher Four Wheel Drive Trail.

SPECIFIC SKILLS RECOMMENDED

Technical skiing
Intermediate at the west end, beginner at the east.

Endurance
Strenuous, assuming that you break trail. The total distance for the loop from Beaver Reservoir is 5.7 miles.

Routefinding
Intermediate.

VIEWS

Nothing in addition to those for the Coney Flats Trail.

PRIVATE PROPERTY AND OTHER RESTRICTIONS

None.

❄ ❄ ❄

TRAIL NO. 10B

CONEY FLATS-MIDDLE ST. VRAIN TRAIL

TRAIL MAP: 5

SUMMARY

Descending from the wind swept meadows of Coney Flats to the towering trees and deep powder snow of the upper Middle St. Vrain valley, this connecting trail joins the Coney Flats Trail with the parallel Middle St. Vrain Road and Buchanan Pass Trail. All three trails that together have penetrated the alpine forest to near timberline and the wilderness boundary are thereby joined at their western limits.

The short, moderately steep descent the trail offers is a welcome respite from the long steady climb on the Coney Flats Trail used to gain access.

CLASSIFICATION: Moderate-difficult.

MAPS (USGS 7.5' quadrangles)

Allens Park (A3)

ELEVATIONS (feet)

Starting....................................9790
Highest....................................9820
Cumulative gain 30
Cumulative loss.........................230

DISTANCE (miles, one way).......0.6

TIME (hours)

Outbound (down) 0.3
Return (up)................................0.5

ACCESS

South end. From the Beaver Reservoir North Trailhead (E), ski the Coney Flats Trail (10),3.2 miles to its end.

North end. From the Peaceful Valley Trailhead (D), ski the Middle St. Vrain Road (6), 4.6 miles to a sign-marked junction.

USAGE

Very light.

SNOW CONDITIONS

Poor where exposed to the wind at Coney Flats but good to excellent in the shelter of the trees elsewhere.

WIND EXPOSURE

Very exposed in the open at Coney Flats, but well protected by large trees thereafter.

GRADIENT

After crossing a nearly flat bench, the trail descends a moderate slope to the valley bottom.

ROUTE DESCRIPTION

From the wilderness boundary and Coney Flats trailhead signs marking the end of the Coney Flats Trail (10), head directly north across the windswept meadow to locate the jeep road pathway cut into the low trees. It becomes more distinct as it enters larger trees and descends to the valley bottom and a junction with the Middle St. Vrain Road (6) at 0.6 miles.

ADDITIONAL CONNECTING TRAIL INFORMATION

None.

SPECIFIC SKILLS RECOMMENDED

Technical skiing
Beginner

Endurance
Strenuous, Beaver Reservoir to Peaceful Valley by this route is 8.4 miles.

Routefinding
Beginner, the only problem could be finding the jeep road at the start when visibility is reduced by blowing snow.

VIEWS

None other than those for the Coney Flats Trail.

PRIVATE PROPERTY AND OTHER RESTRICTIONS

None.

❄ ❄ ❄

TRAIL NO. 11

SOUTH ST. VRAIN TRAIL

TRAIL MAPS: 9, 8, 7

SUMMARY

A wide variety of snow and weather conditions can be encountered in following this aged pack trail as it gains 1700 feet in five and a half miles on its way up South St. Vrain Creek from the Peak to Peak Highway to Brainard Lake.

CLASSIFICATION: Moderate-difficult.

MAPS (USGS 7.5' quadrangles)

Ward (B3)
Gold Hill (B4)

ELEVATIONS (feet)

Starting....................................8740
Highest...................................10480
Cumulative gain 1730
Cumulative loss...........................70

DISTANCE (miles, one way).......5.6

TIME (hours)

Outbound 3.0
Return 2.0

ACCESS

At Tahosa Bridge Trailhead (G).

USAGE

Light.

SNOW CONDITIONS

Conditions at the lower end can be very poor. The upper part will likely be good except in the long meadow at the end where it will usually be blown clear.

WIND EXPOSURE

The trail is for the most part, well protected by trees. The 0.7 mile section from the junction with the Chipmunk Gulch Trail to the Baptist Camp is exposed to the wind, and the final 300 yards in the open meadow at the west end is exposed to strong winds.

GRADIENT

The overall grade is slight, with some short moderate segments.

ROUTE DESCRIPTION

From the Tahosa Bridge Trailhead (G), ski upstream along the west side of South St. Vrain Creek. At 0.9 miles, the trail climbs away from the stream, past a pond and up an aspen covered slope. At 1.6 miles pass a log shelter and at 1.9 miles return to the creek at a low vehicle bridge and an unmarked junction with a road.

Follow the road upstream along the north side of the creek to its end at the buildings of the Baptist Camp at 2.6 miles. Beyond the camp the narrow trail climbs more steeply through thick trees past sign-marked junctions with two trails from the north and on to a sign-marked junction with the Middle Sourdough Trail (12) from the south at 2.9 miles.

The coincident trails are blue diamond blazed where they follow the north side of the creek west to a sign-marked junction at 3.9 miles. Here the blue diamond blazed Middle Sourdough Trail heads north uphill and the South St. Vrain Trail crosses a tributary creek and heads west along a minor ridge staying south of a large meadow. The widely spaced blue diamond blazes continue to 4.6 miles but are visible only for westbound travel. A sign-marked junction with the Waldrop (North) Trail (13), and blue diamond blazes again, is reached at 4.9 miles.

Cross a stream gorge, steep on the west side, 100 yards beyond the junction and continue past a sign-marked junction with the Brainard Bridge Cutoff Trail (13A) at 5.0 miles. At 5.5 miles the trail emerges from the dense trees. A post marks where the Waldrop (North) trail jogs south across the clearing on a blue diamond blazed route. The unblazed South St. Vrain Trail continues west along the north side of the clearing 300 yards to a sign-marked junction with the Mitchell Lake Road Spur (14B) at 5.6 miles.

ADDITIONAL CONNECTING TRAIL INFORMATION

A summary of the junctions with other trails and routes is as follows:
    (1) Chipmunk Gulch Trail (11A) at 1.9 miles.
    (2) Church Camp Cutoff Trail (12B) at 2.7 miles.
    (3) Middle Sourdough Trail (12) at 2.9 miles.
    (4) Middle Sourdough Trail (12) at 3.9 miles.
    (5) Waldrop (North) Trail (13) at 4.9 miles.
    (6) Brainard Bridge Cutoff Trail (13 A) at 5.0 miles.
    (7) Waldrop (North) Trail (13) at 5.5 miles.
    (8) Audubon Cutoff Route (21A) at 5.5 miles.
    (9) Mitchell Lake Road Spur (14B) at 5.6 miles.

SPECIFIC SKILLS RECOMMENDED

Technical skiing
Intermediate.

Endurance
Strenuous.

Routefinding
Intermediate.

VIEWS

The Indian Peaks as viewed from the open meadow at the west end of the trail are from left to right: Kiowa Peak above Niwot Ridge, Navajo Peak, Apache Peak, Shoshoni Peak, Pawnee Peak, Mount Toll, the tip of Paiute Peak, and Mt. Audubon.

PRIVATE PROPERTY AND OTHER RESTRICTIONS

A part of the western end of the trail is within the Indian Peaks Wilderness.

❋ ❋ ❋

TRAIL NO. 11A

CHIPMUNK GULCH TRAIL

TRAIL MAPS: 9, 8

SUMMARY

The central sections of the South St. Vrain and Middle Sourdough trails are reached from the Peak to Peak Highway by this jeep road. It is shorter, easier to ski, and typically has better snow conditions than the lower part of the South St. Vrain trail.

CLASSIFICATION: Easy.

MAPS (USGS 7.5' quadrangles)

Ward (B3)
Gold Hill (B4)

ELEVATIONS (feet)

Starting.....................................9190
Highest......................................9430
Cumulative gain 260
Cumulative loss............................80

DISTANCE (miles, one way).......1.2

TIME (hours)

Outbound 0.8
Return 0.5

ACCESS

At Chipmunk Gulch Trailhead (H)

USAGE

Very light.

SNOW CONDITIONS

Poor where the trail descends to the creek. This section is frequently icy or bare from the exposure to sun and wind. The remainder of the trail is shielded by trees and has medium quality snow.

WIND EXPOSURE

Exposed where the trail descends to the creek.

GRADIENT

Generally nearly flat, with a slight gradient at the descent to the creek.

ROUTE DESCRIPTION

From the highway road cut at the trailhead, take the higher of two jeep roads heading west. The easily followed road climbs past a trailer on the right at 0.2 miles, follows a curving near-level course through thick trees, and then turns left to descend into the open. Take the right fork, pass a silver trailer on your left, and cross the South St. Vrain Creek on a low vehicle bridge at 1.2 miles. Here the trail ends at an unmarked junction with the South St. Vrain Trail (11).

ADDITIONAL CONNECTING TRAIL INFORMATION

None.

SPECIFIC SKILLS RECOMMENDED

Technical skiing
Novice.

Endurance
Very easy.

Routefinding
Novice.

VIEWS

Bounded by Niwot Ridge on the south and Mt. Audubon on the north, the peaks on the continental divide at the head of South St. Vrain Creek are seen from a distance of about seven miles. They are from left to right: Navajo, Apache, Shoshoni, and Pawnee Peaks; Mt. Toll and Mt. Audubon.

Private property is adjacent to the road.

❅ ❅ ❅

TRAIL NO. 12

MIDDLE SOURDOUGH TRAIL

TRAIL MAPS: 8, 7

SUMMARY

This trail, the center section of the long, north to south Sourdough Trail, parallels the Peak to Peak Highway which is one to two miles to the east. An intermediate, blazed trail, it traverses undulating forested terrain from Beaver Reservoir to the Brainard Lake Road at Red Rock Trailhead.

CLASSIFICATION: Moderate-difficult.

MAPS (USGS 7.5' quadrangles)

Ward (B3)

ELEVATIONS (feet)

Starting...................................10060
Highest...................................10120
Cumulative gain 600
Cumulative loss........................1620

DISTANCE (miles, one way).......6.3

TIME (hours)

Outbound (northbound)...............3.1
Return (southbound) 3.5

ACCESS

North end. At Beaver Reservoir East Trailhead (F).
South end. At Red Rock Trailhead (I).

USAGE

Light from Red Rock Trailhead down to and along the South St. Vrain Creek. Very light north of there.

SNOW CONDITIONS

Conditions vary considerably along the trail, primarily with altitude. The southern portion from Red Rock Trailhead down to and along South St. Vrain Creek and about 0.4 miles beyond to where it drops below 10,000 feet altitude has good snow. From there to the switchback at 9,400 feet it is likely of medium quality, and the final 1.7 miles, below 9,400 feet, are frequently poor.

WIND EXPOSURE

The trail is well protected except near the pond at 3.4 miles and at Fresno Lake at 3.9 miles.

GRADIENT

Moderate gradients are interspersed with less steep and nearly flat sections. The steepest is the descent from Red Rock Trailhead to South St. Vrain Creek.

ROUTE DESCRIPTION (South to North)

From the log buck and pole fence near the east end of the Red Rock Trailhead area, ski to the blue diamond tree blaze visible across a meadow 100 yards to the east, and then 100 yards north to a large sign. Enter the trees on a well defined, blue diamond blazed trail, and descend through two switchbacks 400 feet to cross South St. Vrain Creek on a footbridge. A sign-marked junction with the South St. Vrain Trail (11) is 50 yards beyond, at 1.3 miles. The coincident trails climb gently and then more steeply west to a sign-marked junction at 2.4 miles where the South St. Vrain Trail continues west.

The Sourdough Trail climbs to the north and turns east to descend a steep 100 feet to a level area at 3.0 miles. The trail follows the north perimeter of the level area, through low aspen trees close to the low hill to the north. A sign *Baptiste Camp* at an alternate southbound trail is passed at 3.7 miles and the trail continues east along the north side of Fresno Lake at 3.9 miles.
Turning north, the trail descends 160 feet to a sign-marked junction with the Baptiste Trail from the southeast at 4.3 miles. Continue north to a sign-marked junction at 4.6 miles where the Baptiste Trail (12C), continues straight and the Sourdough switchbacks east and downhill. Continue past a crossing of an unplowed road at 5.2 miles and over the low hills, scene of a fire in 1988, to the Beaver Reservoir East Trailhead (F) at 6.3 miles.

ADDITIONAL CONNECTING TRAIL INFORMATION

A sign-marked junction with the Church Camp Cutoff Trail (12B) is at 3.7 miles.

An unmarked junction with the Beaver Reservoir Road Cutoff Trail (12A) is at 5.2 miles.

SPECIFIC SKILLS RECOMMENDED

Technical skiing
Intermediate.

Endurance
Strenuous.

Routefinding
Intermediate.

VIEWS

Niwot Mountain is visible to the south from the level bench near 3.5 miles.

Beaver Reservoir is visible one mile to the north from near the switchback at 4.6 miles.

Mt. Audubon, Sawtooth Mountain, Ogallala Peak, Elk Tooth, and St. Vrain Mountain are visible from a minor ridge crossed at 4.9 miles.

PRIVATE PROPERTY AND OTHER RESTRICTIONS

The Baptiste Trail continues into private property both to the northwest and southeast.

❊ ❊ ❊

TRAIL NO. 12A

BEAVER RESERVOIR ROAD CUTOFF

TRAIL MAP: 8

SUMMARY

This short easy jeep road gives access to the middle section of the Sourdough Trail from the Beaver Reservoir Road. It is particularly useful when the access road is not driveable all the way to the Beaver Reservoir East Trailhead.

CLASSIFICATION: Easy.

MAPS (USGS 7.5' quadrangles)

Ward (B3)

ELEVATIONS (feet)

Starting....................................8920
Highest....................................9160
Cumulative gain 240
Cumulative loss............................0

DISTANCE (miles, one way).......0.7

TIME (hours)

Outbound 0.4
Return 0.3

ACCESS

From the Tahosa Bridge Trailhead (G), drive west on the Beaver Reservoir Road 1.3 miles. Park near the curves where the jeep road is visible to the west. It is marked with a sign, *Forest Service Road 113 A.*

USAGE

Nearly unused.

SNOW CONDITIONS

Usually very poor, although this may not be true if the Beaver Reservoir Road is undriveable due to snow.

WIND EXPOSURE

Moderate due to the thin tree cover.

GRADIENT

Slight.

ROUTE DESCRIPTION

Ski the obvious jeep road up the north side of the drainage to the unmarked junction with the Middle Sourdough Trail (12) at 0.7 miles.

ADDITIONAL CONNECTING TRAIL INFORMATION

The junction with the Middle Sourdough Trail is at mile 5.2 of that trail and is 1.1 miles south of the Beaver Reservoir East Trailhead (F).

SPECIFIC SKILLS RECOMMENDED

Technical skiing
Novice.

Endurance
Very easy.

Routefinding
Novice.

VIEWS

Mt. Audubon and Sawtooth Mountain.

PRIVATE PROPERTY AND OTHER RESTRICTIONS

None.

❄ ❄ ❄

TRAIL NO. 12B

CHURCH CAMP CUTOFF TRAIL

TRAIL MAP: 8

SUMMARY

A rough, locally steep 550 yard trail, it shortcuts a 2.4 mile bend of the Middle Sourdough Trail.

CLASSIFICATION: Moderate-difficult.

MAPS (USGS 7.5' quadrangles)

Ward (B3)

ELEVATIONS (feet)

Starting....................................9640
Highest....................................9720
Cumulative gain 80
Cumulative loss............................0

DISTANCE (miles, one way).......0.3

TIME (hours)

Outbound (northbound)...............0.3
Return (southbound) 0.2

ACCESS

South end. From the junction at mile 1.3 on the Middle Sourdough Trail (12)(50 yards north of the bridge over Middle St. Vrain Creek), ski east on the South St. Vrain Trail (11) 400 yards to a sign-marked junction. This is at mile 2.7 of the South St. Vrain Trail, 200 yards west of the Baptist Camp.

North end. At a sign-marked junction at mile 3.7 of the Sourdough Trail.

USAGE

Nearly unused.

SNOW CONDITIONS

Poor.

WIND EXPOSURE

Very little.

GRADIENT

Moderate at the south end, less steep further north.

ROUTE DESCRIPTION (South to North)

From the westernmost of two sign-marked junctions near mile 2.7 on the South St. Vrain Trail (11), ski north up the initially steep, confined, rocky trail. This soon levels out and joins the Middle Sourdough Trail (12) at 0.3 miles.

ADDITIONAL CONNECTING TRAIL INFORMATION

A second trail to the north, 100 yards further east on the South St. Vrain Trail, joins the trail described here near the midpoint.

SPECIFIC SKILLS RECOMMENDED

Technical skiing
Intermediate.

Endurance
Moderate.

Routefinding
Beginner.

VIEWS

None.

PRIVATE PROPERTY AND OTHER RESTRICTIONS

None.

❋ ❋ ❋

TRAIL NO. 12C

BAPTISTE TRAIL

TRAIL MAP: 8

SUMMARY

This little-used trail traverses a tree-protected route over a mile of easy terrain from the Middle Sourdough Trail to dead end at Stapp Lakes where exit to the north is blocked by private property.

CLASSIFICATION: Moderate.

MAPS (USGS 7.5' quadrangles)

Ward (B3)

ELEVATIONS (feet)

```
Starting...................................9400
Highest....................................9440
Cumulative gain .........................80
Cumulative loss..........................80
```

DISTANCE (miles, one way).......1.0

TIME (hours)

```
Outbound ...................................1.2
Return .......................................0.6
```

ACCESS

From Beaver Reservoir East Trailhead (F), ski south on the Middle Sourdough Trail (12), 1.7 miles to a sign-marked junction at a trail switchback.

USAGE

Nearly unused.

SNOW CONDITIONS

Medium.

WIND EXPOSURE

None.

GRADIENT

Nearly flat.

ROUTE DESCRIPTION

From the sign-marked junction with the Middle Sourdough Trail (12), follow the metal-can blazed route to the northwest on a near-level traverse through the forest. Stay near or slightly onto the steeper slopes to the left when in doubt as to the sometimes faint route. Pass above and to the left of a pond at 0.6 miles and continue to the southernmost of the Stapp Lakes, marked with a sign *No Campfires* at 1.0 miles.

ADDITIONAL CONNECTING TRAIL INFORMATION

None.

SPECIFIC SKILLS RECOMMENDED

Technical skiing
Beginner, deep untracked snow and down trees can create some difficulty.

Endurance
Moderate, again caused by untracked snow.

Routefinding
Intermediate, the square tin can blazes are not always easy to see.

VIEWS

None.

PRIVATE PROPERTY AND OTHER RESTRICTIONS

Exit to the north is blocked by private land near Stapp Lakes.

❀ ❀ ❀

TRAIL NO. 13

WALDROP (NORTH) TRAIL

TRAIL MAPS: 8, 7

SUMMARY

One of the classic trails from Red Rock Trailhead to Brainard Lake, the small but steep gullies encountered on the straight line course of the abandoned telephone line add a bit of excitement not found on the other parallel trails. Coupled with the CMC South or Little Raven Trails it makes a pleasant loop tour of several hours over dependably good snow with a possible warming stop at the Colorado Mountain Club Brainard Cabin. As with the other trails to Brainard, it provides access to the far-reaching skiing beyond.

CLASSIFICATION: Moderate.

MAPS (USGS 7.5' quadrangles)

Ward (B3)

ELEVATIONS (feet)

Starting....................................10120
Highest....................................10420
Cumulative gain 510
Cumulative loss..........................230

DISTANCE (miles, one way).......2.8

TIME (hours)

Outbound 1.4
Return 1.0

ACCESS

At Red Rock Trailhead (I).

USAGE

Moderate.

SNOW CONDITIONS

Medium at the east end, improving to good at the west.

WIND EXPOSURE

Generally well protected by trees, a 100 yard clearing near the midpoint of the trail where it turns north away from the road, is exposed to the wind. A second approximately 100 yard clearing crossed near the far end where the trail splits away from the South St. Vrain Trail is exposed to high winds.

Colorado Mountain Club Brainard Lake cabin

GRADIENT

Slight overall but with moderate gradients at four small gullies crossed by the straight line section following the telephone line and at one larger drainage beyond.

ROUTE DESCRIPTION

From the parking alongside the Brainard Lake Road, walk or ski west on the road 50 yards past the winter closure gate to the sign-marked trailhead on the north side of the road at the first curve. The blue diamond blazed trail makes a wide loop to the north before crossing the outlet creek from Red Rock Lake at 0.6 miles and heading west on a three-quarter mile straight section that relentlessly follows the route of an abandoned telephone line without regard for contours as it crosses four gullies.

Ski 300 yards past a six foot boulder in the middle of the trail to a 100 yard diameter clearing at 1.5 miles. A small sign *To Road,* points to the left here. To continue on the Waldrop (North) Trail, ski across the meadow, descending slightly, cross South St. Vrain Creek at 1.7 miles and climb to a sign-marked junction with the South St. Vrain Trail (11) at 2.1 miles.

Continue 100 yards more to cross a stream gorge, steeper on the far side. Forty yards beyond the top of the climb out is a sign-marked junction with the Brainard Bridge Cutoff Trail (13A) at 2.2 miles. Continue west on a gentle climb and emerge from the dense trees at 2.7 miles to an area of stunted trees and wind sculptured drifts. Turn left (south) to cross the wind swept area, there may be flagging but tracks are quickly obscured by the high winds. On entering the trees again, find the blue diamond blazes and follow the trail west through the trees past the cabin of the Boulder group of the Colorado Mountain Club (CMC), 60 yards to an unmarked junction with the Mitchell Lake Road Spur (14B) at 2.8 miles.

The CMC cabin is usually hosted on weekends during the winter and offers a hot drink and warm resting place to both members and non-members for a small fee.

On the return, the wide loop to the northeast near the eastern end may be shortcut by bushwhacking 100 yards to the road through thick trees anywhere between the top of a slight rise near 0.8 miles and the stream crossing at 0.6 miles.

ADDITIONAL CONNECTING TRAIL INFORMATION

An unblazed trail from the sign at 1.5 miles leads about 200 yards to the Brainard Lake Road (14), as does an unmarked jeep road 100 yards to the west.

Sign-marked junctions with the South St. Vrain Trail (11), are at 2.1 miles, 100 yards before a stream gorge, and at 2.7 miles, at the entrance to a wind-swept meadow. Between these two points, the trails are coincident.

A sign-marked junction with the Brainard Bridge Cutoff Trail (13A), is at 2.2 miles, 60 yards west of the top of the stream gorge.

An unmarked junction with the Audubon Cutoff Route (21A), is at 2.7 miles.

SPECIFIC SKILLS RECOMMENDED

Technical skiing
Intermediate, the gullies can be challenging for the beginner.

Endurance
Easy.

Routefinding
Novice, the well traveled trail is distinct and blazed with blue diamonds.

VIEWS

Longs Peak and Mt. Meeker are visible to the north from a clearing near the stream crossing at 0.6 miles.

PRIVATE PROPERTY AND OTHER RESTRICTIONS

Dogs are not permitted. A section of the western portion of the trail is within the Indian Peaks Wilderness.

❄ ❄ ❄

TRAIL NO. 13A

BRAINARD BRIDGE CUTOFF TRAIL

TRAIL MAP: 7

SUMMARY

This short, easy, and well-protected cutoff trail from the Waldrop (North) and South St. Vrain Trails to Brainard Lake avoids the wind swept meadow they both encounter further west.

CLASSIFICATION: Easy.

MAPS (USGS 7.5' quadrangles)

Ward (B3)

ELEVATIONS (feet)

```
Starting.................................10300
Highest.................................10380
Cumulative gain ..........................80
Cumulative loss...........................40
```

DISTANCE (miles, one way).......0.5

TIME (hours)

```
Outbound ....................................0.3
Return .........................................0.3
```

ACCESS

East end. From Red Rock Trailhead (I), ski the Waldrop (North) Trail (13) 2.2 miles to the sign-marked junction.

West end. Brainard Lake Trailhead (R), at the northwest end of the bridge.

USAGE

Very light.

SNOW CONDITIONS

Good.

WIND EXPOSURE

Well protected except at the lake.

GRADIENT

Nearly flat.

ROUTE DESCRIPTION

The northeast end of the trail at the junction with the Waldrop (North) (13) and South St. Vrain (11) Trails is marked with a sign *Brainard Lake.* This is 60 yards west of the top of the stream gorge at mile 2.2 on the Waldrop (North) Trail. White diamond trail blazes mark the trail to the northwest end of the bridge over the outlet stream at the east end of Brainard Lake. The trail junction here is marked with a sign *Waldrop Trail, 1 mile.*

ADDITIONAL CONNECTING TRAIL INFORMATION

None.

SPECIFIC SKILLS RECOMMENDED

Technical skiing
Novice.

Endurance
Easy.

Routefinding
Beginner.

VIEWS

None.

PRIVATE PROPERTY AND OTHER RESTRICTIONS

None.

❄ ❄ ❄

TRAIL NO. 14, 14A, 14B, 14C

BRAINARD LAKE ROAD (14)
BRAINARD LAKE ROAD LOOP (14 A)
MITCHELL LAKE ROAD SPUR (14 B)
LONG LAKE ROAD SPUR (14 C)

TRAIL MAPS: 8, 7

SUMMARY

The Brainard Lake Road continues past the winter closure gate at the Red Rock Trailhead west two miles to Brainard Lake. A nearly flat, wide paved road, stretches of it are frequently blown clear of snow. It can serve as an emergency escape route from the Brainard Lake area as it can be followed at night or in ground blizzards when traveling downwind (east). It can probably be done without skis without much difficulty.

The loop road circles the lake and the spur roads connect with trails extending west.

CLASSIFICATION: Easy.

MAPS (USGS 7.5' quadrangles)

Ward (B3)

ELEVATIONS (feet)

```
Starting.................................10300
Highest..................................10500
Cumulative gain
Red Rock to lake.......................290
To west side, add .........................40
Mitchell spur, add .......................110
Long spur, add ...........................120
Cumulative loss..............................0
```

DISTANCE (miles, one way)

```
Red Rock to lake..........................2.1
To west side, add ........................0.5
Either spur, add...........................0.4
```

TIME (hours, either direction)

```
Red Rock to lake..........................1.2
To west side, add ........................0.2
Either spur, add..........................0.2
```

ACCESS

At Red Rock Trailhead (I).

USAGE

Heavy.

SNOW CONDITIONS

Generally poor due to the wind. Some sections, especially on the spur trails are rated medium.

WIND EXPOSURE

These unprotected roads are exposed to the effects of the high winds that are common in the area. Expect hard wind-packed snow, bare areas where the snow has been blown away, reduced visibility in ground blizzards, and the possibility of frostbite to exposed skin.

GRADIENT

Nearly flat.

ROUTE DESCRIPTION

The wide paved road continues west from the winter closure gate at the Red Rock Trailhead (I) to Brainard Lake at 2.1 miles. As the lake is approached, continue straight on the old road which now provides summer access to a campground or jog south on the main road. Follow the Brainard Lake Loop Road (14A) around the lake in either direction to the junction with the spur roads, marked with a road sign. The common spur road divides in 200 yards, with the Mitchell Lake Road Spur (14B) continuing straight while the Long Lake Road Spur (14C) turns to the left. Both continue 0.4 mile to end at summer parking lots.

ADDITIONAL CONNECTING TRAIL INFORMATION

An unmarked 100 yard bushwhacking route to the Waldrop (North) Trail (13) may be done west of the outlet creek of Red Rock Lake, crossed at 0.5 miles.
A blue diamond blazed route south to the CMC South Trail (15) is marked by a sign at 1.3 miles.

An unmarked trail at 1.4 miles as well as a jeep road 100 yards further west provide access north to the Waldrop (North) Trail (13).

A sign post marks the junction with the CMC South (15) and Little Raven (16) Trails at a brushy clearing at the southwest corner of the Brainard Lake Loop Road (14A). About 200 yards north on the loop road ,and across from a toilet, is the sign-marked junction with the Long Lake Cutoff Trail (24).

A sign *Waldrop Trail 1 mile* marks the junction with the Brainard Bridge Cutoff Trail (13A) at the northwest end of the bridge across the outlet creek on the northeast shore.

The Mitchell-Blues Lakes Trail (20) and the Beaver Creek Trail (21) both begin at the end of the Mitchell Lake Road Spur (14B). The Pawnee Pass Trail (22) continues on from the end of the Long Lake Road Spur (14C).

SPECIFIC SKILLS RECOMMENDED

Technical skiing
Novice.

Endurance
Very easy for the Brainard Lake Road, Easy for the loop and road spurs.

Routefinding
Novice.

VIEWS

Unobstructed views from the wide road are of the Indian Peaks on the continental divide. These are at the head of the South St. Vrain Valley and are bounded by Niwot Ridge on the south and Mt. Audubon on the north. They are from left to right: Navajo, Apache, Shoshoni, and Pawnee Peaks, Mt. Toll, Paiute Peak, and Mt. Audubon.

PRIVATE PROPERTY AND OTHER RESTRICTIONS

None, this is the only trail west from the Red Rock Trailhead on which dogs are permitted.

❄ ❄ ❄

TRAIL NO. 15

CMC SOUTH

TRAIL MAPS: 8, 7

SUMMARY

This, the easiest of the trails extending west from Red Rock Trailhead, follows an abandoned ditch on a contour route through dense timber much of the way to Brainard Lake. Coupled with the Waldrop (North) Trail, it makes a enjoyable loop trip with a warming stop at the CMC Brainard Cabin. The more ambitious continue on the multitude of trails west from Brainard.

CLASSIFICATION: Easy.

MAPS (USGS 7.5' quadrangles)

Ward (B3)

ELEVATIONS (feet)

Starting................................10120
Highest................................10420
Cumulative gain 360
Cumulative loss..........................60

DISTANCE (miles, one way).......2.2

TIME (hours)

Outbound 1.1
Return 0.9

ACCESS

At Red Rock Trailhead (I).

USAGE

Heavy.

SNOW CONDITIONS

Good.

WIND EXPOSURE

Generally well protected by trees, a few open meadows are exposed along the way. It is exposed at the far end in the brushy clearing where it joins the Brainard Lake Loop Road.

Mt. Toll, Paiute Peak, and Mt. Audubon from Boulder

GRADIENT

Nearly flat except for a short moderate sections near the start and at 1.8 miles.

ROUTE DESCRIPTION

The blue diamond blazed trail branches off left at the first curve of the Brainard Lake Road (14), at a trail sign 50 yards west of the winter closure gate. It immediately climbs a short moderate slope. Much of the remainder of the trail follows the contouring route of a ditch. Ski past the chimney remnants of summer cabins to a junction with the Little Raven Trail (16), marked with a stone and bronze monument honoring Chief Little Raven, and 70 yards more across a brushy clearing to the junction with the Brainard Lake Loop Road (14A) at 2.2 miles.

CONNECTIONS WITH OTHER TRAILS AND ROUTES

A sign-marked junction with an 80 yard unblazed connecting trail to the Left Hand Park Reservoir Road (17) is in a 20 yard diameter clearing 150 yards beyond the top of the climb at the start of the trail.

At 1.1 miles a trail sign marks a junction with a blue diamond blazed trail leading 300 yards north to the Brainard Lake Road (14).

At 2.0 miles, where the dam at the east end of Brainard Lake is visible through the trees to the north, the Brainard Loop Road (14A) is only 100 yards distant.

Junctions with the Little Raven Trail (16) and Brainard Lake Loop Road (14A) are at the end of the trail at 2.2 miles.

SPECIFIC SKILLS RECOMMENDED

Technical skiing
Beginner.

Endurance
Very easy.

Routefinding
Novice.

VIEWS

None.

PRIVATE PROPERTY AND OTHER RESTRICTIONS

Posted Forest Service regulations prohibit dogs on the trail.

❄ ❄ ❄

TRAIL NO. 16

LITTLE RAVEN TRAIL

TRAIL MAPS: 8, 7

SUMMARY

The most recently built of the trails from Red Rock Trailhead to Brainard Lake, it has more difficult terrain and generally the least use and best snow. The steep eastern part of the trail can be bypassed using the Left Hand Park Reservoir Road.

CLASSIFICATION: Moderate-difficult.

MAPS (USGS 7.5' quadrangles)

Ward (B3)

ELEVATIONS (feet)

Starting..................................10040
Highest..................................10580
Cumulative gain 540
Cumulative loss..........................200

DISTANCE (miles, one way).......2.7

TIME (hours)

Outbound 1.5
Return 0.9

ACCESS

From the Red Rock Trailhead (I), ski south on the South Sourdough Trail (18), 0.4 miles to a sign-marked junction.

USAGE

Light.

SNOW CONDITIONS

Snow quality will likely be good beyond the ponds and meadows along Left Hand Creek which is crossed midway along the trail. Prior to that, on the road and along the exposed drainage, the snow suffers from the effects of the wind and sun.

WIND EXPOSURE

Exposed on road and along Left Hand Creek.

GRADIENT

The section from the beginning to the Left Hand Park Reservoir Road at 0.6 miles is a steep narrow path through trees. Beyond there, the slope is slight to moderate.

ROUTE DESCRIPTION

From the sign-marked junction on the South Sourdough Trail (18), climb the steep, narrow, blue diamond blazed trail through trees 0.6 mile to the Left Hand Park Reservoir Road (17) at a sign-marked junction. Follow the road on a gradual climb southwest. At 1.0 miles, leave the road at a sign and head west on a near level, unblazed but distinct trail cut through trees 300 yards to the clearing along Left Hand Creek. Blue diamond blazes mark a route through the treeless area, first to the right and then back left upstream and into the trees.

A long traverse and easy descent to a junction with the CMC South Trail (15) at

2.7 miles is marked with blue diamond blazes. Here a stone and bronze monument honors Chief Little Raven. The Brainard Lake Loop Road (14A) is 70 yards northwest across a brushy meadow.

CONNECTIONS WITH OTHER TRAILS AND ROUTES

The trail is coincident with the Left Hand Park Reservoir Road (17) for 0.4 miles.

SPECIFIC SKILLS RECOMMENDED

Technical skiing
Intermediate.

Endurance
Easy.

Routefinding
Novice.

VIEWS

Unobstructed views of the Indian Peaks are obtained from the clearing along Left Hand Creek and from the road. The individual peaks are the same as listed for the Left Hand Park Reservoir Road (17).

PRIVATE PROPERTY AND OTHER RESTRICTIONS

Dogs are not allowed on the Little Raven Trail.

❄ ❄ ❄

TRAIL NO. 17

LEFT HAND PARK RESERVOIR ROAD

TRAIL MAP: 8

SUMMARY

Sometimes offering packed slopes reminiscent of a downhill ski area and at other times a rocky roadbed, this wide, moderately steep road climbs from Red Rock Trailhead, 550 feet to the nearly always windy reservoir. The lower part can be used to avoid the steep eastern part of the Little Raven Trail or even to avoid the short hill at the beginning of the CMC South Trail.

CLASSIFICATION: Moderate.

MAPS (USGS 7.5' quadrangles)

Ward (B3)

ELEVATIONS (feet)

```
Starting..................................10070
Highest...................................10620
Cumulative gain .........................550
Cumulative loss..............................0
```

DISTANCE (miles, one way).......1.7

TIME (hours)

```
Outbound ....................................1.0
Return ........................................0.6
```

ACCESS

At the Red Rock Trailhead (I).

USAGE

Moderate.

SNOW CONDITIONS

Poor, exposed corners on the lower part of the road may be blown clear of snow. The final 0.4 mile is frequently blown clear of snow.

WIND EXPOSURE

The moderate exposure of this wide road to wind increases to extreme for the final 0.4 mile to the reservoir.

GRADIENT

The gradient from about 0.4 miles to the junction with the Little Raven Trail at 0.9 miles is moderate. Gradients above and below are less steep.

ROUTE DESCRIPTION

Starting from a sign-marked junction on the Brainard Lake Road, there are no problems in following this wide road through trees. Cross Left Hand Creek on a vehicle bridge at 0.8 miles and pass the sign marked junction where the Little Raven Trail branches off to the right at 1.2 miles. Beyond here, tracks will usually be found along the northwest side of the road where skiers have sought shelter from the high winds in the scrubby trees present there.

The road ends in a large cleared area below the dam near a large sign. The location of this can be helpful in finding the road for the return in periods of poor visibility due to blowing snow.

ADDITIONAL CONNECTING TRAIL INFORMATION

At 0.4 miles, where the road curves left, a trail sign marks a link to the CMC

South Trail (15) which can be made by following a distinct but unblazed jeep trail 80 yards to the right.

A sign at 0.9 miles, 120 yards beyond a vehicle bridge, marks a junction with the Little Raven Trail (16) to the east. The same trail forks off to the west at a sign-marked junction at 1.2 miles and the trails are coincident between.

Ending at the reservoir, the road here makes an unmarked connection with the Niwot Ridge Traverse Route (19A).

SPECIFIC SKILLS RECOMMENDED

Technical skiing
Beginner.

Endurance
Easy.

Routefinding
Novice.

VIEWS

A spectacular view of the Indian Peaks on the continental divide greets the skier at the reservoir. They are (from left to right): Kiowa and Arikaree peaks, a straight section of Niwot Ridge, Navajo, Apache, Shoshoni and Pawnee Peaks, Mt. Toll, Paiute Peak and Mt. Audubon.

PRIVATE PROPERTY AND OTHER RESTRICTIONS

None

❄ ❄ ❄

TRAIL NO. 18

SOUTH SOURDOUGH TRAIL

TRAIL MAPS: 8, 11

SUMMARY

After crossing the steep forested eastern flank of Niwot Mountain on a near level traverse south from Red Rock Trailhead, the trail drops a thousand feet to the Mountain Research Station Trailhead. It can be an enjoyable trip done one way (north to south) with a car shuttle, or as part of a loop trip over Niwot Ridge.

CLASSIFICATION: Moderate-difficult.

MAPS (USGS 7.5' quadrangles)

Ward (B3)

ELEVATIONS (feet)

Starting.....................................10060
Highest.....................................10260
Cumulative gain 450
Cumulative loss.......................1260

DISTANCE (miles, one way).......5.5

TIME (hours)

Outbound (southbound) 2.5
Return (northbound)....................3.1

ACCESS

North end. At Red Rock Trailhead (I).

South end. At a sign-marked trailhead on the plowed road to the University of Colorado Mountain Research Station, 0.4 miles from the highway turn-off. Parking is an additional 0.4 miles along the road to where the unplowed Rainbow Lakes Road (25) turns off.

USAGE

Light.

SNOW CONDITIONS

Poor.

WIND EXPOSURE

Very little.

GRADIENT

Only slight gradients are encountered before the moderate slope near the switchbacks at the head of Fourmile Creek at 3.0 miles. Additional moderate slopes occur near the south end of the trail.

ROUTE DESCRIPTION

From the sign-marked trailhead near the log buck and pole fence, follow the near-level blue diamond blazed trail as it contours along the east side of Niwot Mountain. Switchback left in the trees before entering a gully at the head of Fourmile Creek and again in 100 yards and cross the Peace Memorial Footbridge at 3.0 miles.

Descend gradually to a trail sign at 4.0 miles and take the left, slightly descending fork to cross a gully below an abandoned sawmill site at 4.2 miles. Descend steeply down the fall line on an abandoned logging road which parallels the Niwot Ridge Road and angle left into the trees 130 yards beyond a power line at 4.4

89

miles. The blazed trail jogs to the north to an overlook of Fourmile Creek at 4.8 miles where it turns southeast to follow a barbed wire fence to 5.2 miles and on to the sign-marked trailhead at the plowed road at 5.5 miles.

ADDITIONAL CONNECTING TRAIL INFORMATION

To intercept the Niwot Ridge Road (19) as high as feasible for a trip to the west or possibly a loop trip around Niwot Mountain, take the higher trail at the sign marked junction at 4.0 miles and continue on a near level route between two abandoned buildings and across a meadow 100 yards to the road at 4.2 miles. A 0.4 mile section of plowed road from the south trailhead to the parking area connects to the Rainbow Lakes Road (25)

SPECIFIC SKILLS RECOMMENDED

Technical skiing
Beginner.

Endurance
Strenuous.

Routefinding
Novice.

VIEWS

A saddle at 0.6 miles provides views of Ward, Green Mountain, Bear Peak, Mt. Thoridin, and the plains to the east. The overlook at 4.8 miles furnishes a view of the head of Fourmile Creek and the Peak to Peak highway.

PRIVATE PROPERTY AND OTHER RESTRICTIONS

Skiers should stay on the established Sourdough Trail in the vicinity of the Niwot Ridge Road. Other ski and snowmobile trails provide access to experiments within the Niwot Ridge Biosphere Reserve of the University of Colorado.

❄ ❄ ❄

TRAIL NO. 19

NIWOT RIDGE ROAD

TRAIL MAP: 11

SUMMARY

Extending west from the south end of the South Sourdough Trail above the University of Colorado Mountain Research Station, this pleasant forested trail can be continued to the wind-swept slopes of Niwot Ridge and beyond. It may be part of a loop tour around Niwot Mountain.

CLASSIFICATION: Moderate-difficult.

MAPS (USGS 7.5' quadrangles)

Ward (B3)

ELEVATIONS (feet)

Starting.....................................9800
Highest 11000
Cumulative gain........................1140
Cumulative loss.............................0

DISTANCE (miles, one way).......2.7

TIME (hours)

Outbound 1.9
Return 1.0

ACCESS

From the Mountain Research Station Trailhead (J), ski 1.2 miles north on the South Sourdough Trail (18), gaining 600 feet to where the trail contours into a major gully. Detour 50 yards south through trees to the Niwot Ridge Road.

USAGE

Light.

Windswept Niwot Ridge

SNOW CONDITIONS

Medium overall, good in the protection of trees, but poor where exposed.

WIND EXPOSURE

A significant part of the road is exposed to wind.

GRADIENT

The gradient is never more than moderate, but is unrelenting.

ROUTE DESCRIPTION

On reaching the road from the South Sourdough Trail (18), proceed up the road as it climbs a steep rise and crosses above the sawmill gully, to a level meadow at 0.2 miles. Continue west up the road, past a weather station and trailer at 0.4 miles and 9,960 feet altitude. The road climbs steadily to timberline at 2.7 miles and 11,000 feet altitude. Trails paralleling parts of the road may offer alternative routes with better snow.

ADDITIONAL CONNECTING TRAIL INFORMATION

An unmarked junction with the South Sourdough Trail (18) is in the meadow above the sawmill gully at 0.2 miles. Southbound skiers on the South Sourdough Trail can use this 0.2 mile shortcut and avoid giving up altitude needlessly.

The Niwot Ridge Traverse Route (19A) continues over Niwot Ridge from the end of this road.

SPECIFIC SKILLS RECOMMENDED

Technical skiing
Beginner.

Endurance
Moderate.

Routefinding
Beginner.

VIEWS

North and South Arapaho Peaks; the peaks of the City of Boulder's watershed, Mt. Albion, Kiowa and Arikaree Peaks; and Navajo Peak are visible to the west on the continental divide.

PRIVATE PROPERTY AND OTHER RESTRICTIONS

The City of Boulder watershed is to the south. Heavy fines have been imposed for trespass.

❄ ❄ ❄

TRAIL NO. 19A

NIWOT RIDGE TRAVERSE ROUTE

TRAIL MAPS: 10, 7, 8

SUMMARY

Crossing over wind-swept Niwot Ridge, this untracked route connects the Niwot Ridge Road from the Mountain Research Station Trailhead to the south with the Left Hand Park Reservoir Road from Red Rock Trailhead. An eleven mile loop trip around Niwot Mountain uses this as the high link.

CLASSIFICATION: Difficult.

MAPS (USGS 7.5' quadrangles)

Ward (B3)

ELEVATIONS (feet)

Starting 11000
Highest 11440
Cumulative gain 440
Cumulative loss 840

DISTANCE (miles, one way) 2.4

TIME (hours)

Outbound (northbound) 1.7
Return (southbound) 2.0

ACCESS

South end. From the Mountain Research Station Trailhead (J), ski 1.2 miles on the South Sourdough Trail (18), to an unmarked junction with the Niwot Ridge Road (19). This is then skied 2.7 miles to its end. A total distance of 3.9 miles.

North end. From the Red Rock Trailhead (I), ski the Left Hand Park Reservoir Road (17), 1.7 miles to its end at the reservoir.

USAGE

Nearly unused.

SNOW CONDITIONS

Poor, the ridge crest is frequently blown clear of snow and the snowpack is usually hard wind slab or sculptured sastrugi.

The lake ice is normally free of snow cover. Normally the south bank of the lake is to be preferred as it is difficult to keep ones balance on the lake ice.

WIND EXPOSURE

The entire route is very exposed to wind. The most sheltered site is amongst the scattered clumps of trees at the west end of the lake.

GRADIENT

Uniformly moderate to steep. The extreme width of the slope above Left Hand Park Reservoir makes long traverses possible on the descent.

Niwot Ridge traverse

ROUTE DESCRIPTION

From the end of the identifiable Niwot Ridge Road (19), continue northwest on an easy climb through scattered trees past a weather station trailer. Turn north and climb the wind-packed slope to cross Niwot Ridge at 0.5 miles at a saddle near Point 11,442. This is about 400 yards east of a small research station building on the ridgeline visible from below.

Left Hand Park Reservoir is visible from the ridge, 800 feet below. In poor visibility, following the fall line will lead to the west end of the lake. Cross to the east end and dam at 2.4 miles, going either across the ice or along the south shoreline. Here a large sign below the dam marks the west end of the Left Hand Park Reservoir Road (17), which continues on to Red Rock Trailhead (I).

ADDITIONAL CONNECTING TRAIL INFORMATION

A 11.0 mile loop trip around Niwot Mountain from Red Rock Trailhead (I) utilizes the South Sourdough Trail (18), Niwot Ridge Road (19), and Left Hand Park Reservoir Road (17) along with this route.

SPECIFIC SKILLS RECOMMENDED

Technical skiing
Intermediate skill is recommended to be able to ski difficult snow conditions.

Endurance
Strenuous.

Routefinding
Advanced if visibility is poor.

VIEWS

An outstanding view extends to the south as far as James Peak and Pikes Peak. Closer in are the Indian Peaks; South and North Arapaho, Mt. Albion, Kiowa, Arikaree, and Navajo Peaks. Close to the north are Mt. Toll, Paiute Peak, and Mt. Audubon. Mt. Meeker and Longs Peak dominate the peaks in Rocky Mountain National Park further north.

PRIVATE PROPERTY AND OTHER RESTRICTIONS

None.

❄ ❄ ❄

TRAIL NO. 20

MITCHELL-BLUE LAKES TRAIL

TRAIL MAP: 7

SUMMARY

At the heart of the Indian Peaks Wilderness, summer or winter, and of this guidebook, this trail characterizes skiing the eastern slope of the Front Range better than any other. Crowded on week ends, the Red Rock Trailhead can be reached from Boulder in 45 minutes and Brainard Lake and the start of this trail in little more than an another hour. After a possible warming stop at the CMC Brainard Lake Cabin, other skiers are largely left behind as the trail climbs in deep powder snow through stands of towering Engleman spruce. These yield to more open slopes, playgrounds for telemarking, and then to the harsh wind-swept slopes of incredible beauty amongst the cirques at the base of the high peaks.

CLASSIFICATION: Difficult.

MAPS (USGS 7.5' quadrangles)

Ward (B3)
Monarch Lake (B2)

ELEVATIONS (feet)

Starting................................10480
Highest.................................11320
Cumulative gain 840
Cumulative loss............................0

DISTANCE (miles, one way).......2.3

TIME (hours)

Outbound 1.7
Return 1.0

ACCESS

From the Brainard Lake Trailhead (R), ski the Mitchell Lake Road Spur (14B), 0.4 miles to its end at the summer parking lot. A total skiing distance of 3.0 miles from the car at Red Rock Trailhead (I).

USAGE

Light.

SNOW CONDITIONS

Excellent.

WIND EXPOSURE

Exposure to wind is significant in the treeless area east of Mitchell and Little Mitchell Lakes and above timberline as Blue Lake is approached.

GRADIENT

The steepest of the moderate gradients encountered is in the gully above Mitchell Lake.

ROUTE DESCRIPTION

From the sign-marked trailhead at the Mitchell Lake trail summer parking lot, follow the blue diamond blazed trail to where it turns left near a distinctive brown stained 8 foot stump at 0.3 miles. Continue straight here, picking a route through clearings up the valley to Little Mitchell Lake and over a windswept knoll to Mitchell Lake at 0.8 miles. Cross the outlet and ski westward in the shelter of trees along the south side of the lake to the inlet of Mitchell Creek at 1.0 miles.

Climb the moderately steep treeless gorge to the wide gentle valley above. Select a route over the open slopes and through scattered clumps of trees up the valley to Blue Lake at 2.3 miles. Stay away from avalanche danger at the base of the steep slopes to the south.

ADDITIONAL CONNECTING TRAIL INFORMATION

An alternative route as far as Mitchell Lake follows the summer trail and is less exposed to wind but is difficult to follow unless tracked. Trailbreaking in the loose powder amongst the trees can be strenuous. From the left turn at 0.3 miles, cross Mitchell Creek on a footbridge in 120 yards. The blue diamond blazes end at the sign-marked wilderness boundary 50 yards beyond here. The trail switchbacks in 150 yards more to climb to Mitchell Lake.

Long undulating slopes with scattered lofty trees and legendary powder snow characterize the choice telemarking area known locally as *Hero Hill* at the northwest end of Mitchell Lake. An alternate route can be followed from here to join the gully route a half mile further up.

SPECIFIC SKILLS RECOMMENDED

Technical skiing
Intermediate.

Endurance
Strenuous.

Routefinding
Intermediate.

VIEWS

Little Pawnee and Pawnee Peaks, Mt. Toll, Paiute Peak, and Mt. Audubon tower above Blue Lake.

PRIVATE PROPERTY AND OTHER RESTRICTIONS

All but the eastern 0.3 mile of the route is within the Indian Peaks Wilderness.

❄ ❄ ❄

TRAIL NO. 21

BEAVER CREEK TRAIL

TRAIL MAPS: 7, 5

SUMMARY

One of the premier routes of the area—remote, challenging, arduous, and adventurous. It combines travel on established forest trails with bushwhacking through thick timber, the freedom of above timberline wandering and skiing untouched silent trails through towering trees. This is a high-level route from Brainard Lake to Coney Flats. Combined with one of the trails providing access to Brainard Lake and the Coney Flats Trail at the north end, it affords a ten mile link on the fringe of timberline from Red Rock Trailhead to Beaver Reservoir.

CLASSIFICATION: Very difficult

MAPS (USGS 7.5' quadrangles)

Allens Park (A3)
Ward (B3)

ELEVATIONS (feet)

Starting (Brainard)..................10500
Highest 11320
Cumulative gain 820
Cumulative loss.......................1540

DISTANCE (miles, one way).......4.4

TIME (hours)
Northbound 4.0
Southbound................................4.0

ACCESS

South end—From the Brainard Lake Trailhead (R), ski the Mitchell Lake Road Spur (14B), 0.4 miles to its end at the summer parking lot. A total skiing distance of 3.0 miles from the car at Red Rock Trailhead (I).

North end—From Beaver Reservoir, North Trailhead (E), ski the Coney Flats Trail (10) west 2.6 miles to where the open slopes south of Coney Flats are accessible.

USAGE

Nearly unused

SNOW CONDITIONS

Snow conditions can be expected to range from poor to excellent. Above timberline slopes may have bare tundra, rocks, sastrugi, and wind slab. The switchbacks at 0.8 miles are on a steep south-facing side slope and may be icy. Snow on the trail through the large trees north of Beaver Creek will likely be deep powder and untracked.

WIND EXPOSURE

The 1.9 mile section from the switchbacks at 0.8 miles to where the shelter of trees is regained on the north side of Beaver Creek is exposed to frequent high winds. The open slopes near the junction with the Coney Flats Trail (10) are likewise exposed.

GRADIENT

Generally moderate but with a very steep section on the switchbacks at 0.7 miles, steep slopes on the descent into Beaver Creek drainage and steep open slopes at the junction with the Coney Flats Trail (10) at 4.4 miles.

Snow plumes on north slopes of Mt. Audubon

ROUTE DESCRIPTION

The trailhead is marked with a sign *Beaver Creek Trail* at the northwest corner of the summer Mitchell Lake parking lot. The unblazed trail climbs to the northwest through large Engleman Spruce with two switchbacks not shown on the topographic map. This leads to a clearing at the base of a steep slope at 0.7 miles and 10,840 feet. The slope to the west is a boulder field, to the north is a swath of trees up the slope, and to the east the slope is tree covered. (If you are southbound, on arrival here go west to the center of the 70 yard wide bowl, then south into a small gully which leads to the trail in the trees.)

Continue northbound by heading east on a climbing traverse into the switchbacks. The steep side slope here may be icy and the snow cover windslab. It may be easier to detour to the east of the summer trail where the slope lessens up higher. Climb north through the low brush above timberline to the low saddle, marked with a cairn and signpost at 1.6 miles, the junction with the summer Mt. Audubon trail. This saddle is approximately 100 yards west of a small knoll.

Continue north from the saddle down into the low trees and brush of the Beaver Creek drainage. Pass through a large (200 by 600 yard) clearing in the drainage bottom at 2.7 miles and on through a series of small clearings and dense trees to reach the top of a second large clearing 200 yards in diameter at 10,440 feet. Point 10,964 on the Audubon Cutoff Route (21A) is visible on the skyline to the south from here as is the 200 by 600 yard clearing to the southwest.

At the base of the clearing (10,390 feet), contour out to the northwest, following a tongue of the clearing and continue another 100 yards to intercept the summer trail in the sparse to moderately dense trees here. An alternate easier

99

and higher route to the summer trail contours out at the base of the 200 yard by 600 yard clearing. The summer trail here however, is in an area of thinner trees and more difficult to recognize. Continue north on the now easy to follow trail through large trees to cross a drainage tributary to Beaver Creek at 3.3 miles.

Continue north on the Beaver Creek Trail to arrive at the top of open telemark slopes at 3.9 miles. The summer trail is difficult to follow north to Coney Flats from here through the widely scattered trees. A better alternative is to descend the open slopes and follow the minor drainage northeast to intercept the Coney Flats Trail (10) at 4.4 miles. It is 2.6 miles east to Beaver Reservoir North Trailhead (E).

ADDITIONAL CONNECTING TRAIL INFORMATION

The unmarked junction with the Audubon Cutoff Trail (21A) is at the midpoint of the 200 by 600 yard clearing at 2.7 miles and 10,760 feet altitude.

The unmarked junction with the Firebreak Cutoff Trail (21B) is at the crossing of a drainage at 3.3 miles. The west end of the 20 yard wide firebreak is 200 yards east down the drainage.

An emergency exit to Beaver Reservoir could be made here by going down the wide swath of the firebreak and continuing east on easy terrain through the private property at Stapp Lakes.

SPECIFIC SKILLS RECOMMENDED

Technical skiing
Expert. The switchbacks at 0.7 miles and the above timberline section require good technique and equipment. Climbing skins, metal edges, and ski-mountaineering boots are recommended. The switchbacks are more difficult southbound (downhill).

Endurance
Very strenuous. The total distance including the connecting trails is 10.0 miles with 1330 feet altitude gained and 2240 lost on a south to north passage. Probably all of the 4.4 miles of the Beaver Creek Trail will be untracked, with deep powder in the trees, hard wind-packed snow above timberline, and ice likely on the switchbacks.

Routefinding
Expert. Maps, compass, and altimeter are recommended along with an early start, good weather and capable companions. The routefinding is more difficult southbound due to the difficulty in recognizing the untracked trail in the area of sparse trees and open slopes above the junction with the Coney Flats Trail (10).

VIEWS

From the top of the switchbacks at 0.7 miles the view to the south includes Niwot Mountain, the slopes above Left Hand Park Reservoir crossed by the Niwot Ridge Traverse Route (19A), Mt. Albion, Kiowa and Arikaree Peaks.

At the saddle near the junction of the Mt. Audubon trail (1.6 miles), views to the north and east are similar to those listed for the Audubon Cutoff Route (21A). The nearly flat terrain with scattered clumps of trees traversed by the Audubon Cutoff Route is visible below and 700 yards to the southeast. The view to the west on a windless day is of the above-timberline slopes of Mt. Audubon.

PRIVATE PROPERTY AND OTHER RESTRICTIONS

Exit by the Firebreak Cutoff (21B) to Beaver Reservoir via Stapp Lakes is suggested only as an emergency route. Property at Stapp Lakes is privately owned and trespass is prohibited.

Dogs are not allowed on the Waldrop (North) (13), CMC South (15), nor Little Raven (16) Trails which provide access to the south end of the route.

South of Beaver Creek, the route is within the Indian Peaks Wilderness; to the north, the trail is the eastern boundary.

❄ ❄ ❄

TRAIL NO. 21A

AUDUBON CUTOFF ROUTE

TRAIL MAP: 7

SUMMARY

An alternative to the southern 2.7 miles of the Beaver Creek Trail (21), it avoids the climb and descent of 370 feet of altitude as well as avoiding the steep icy switchbacks and the extended exposure above timberline of that trail. From near the west end of the South St. Vrain or Waldrop (North) Trails, a compass course north through large trees with good snow leads to a bushwhack up a steep slope and finally a climbing traverse and descent through the tree clumps and clearings common near timberline to a junction with the Beaver Creek Trail.

CLASSIFICATION: Very difficult

MAPS (USGS 7.5' quadrangles)

Ward (B3)

ELEVATIONS (feet)

Starting (south) 10450
Highest..............................10970
Cumulative gain 540
Cumulative loss.....................590

DISTANCE (miles, one way).......2.0

TIME (hours)

Outbound 2.1

ACCESS

From Red Rock Trailhead (I), ski the Waldrop (North) Trail (13) 2.7 miles to east end of a wind swept clearing.

From Brainard Lake Trailhead (R), ski 0.3 miles northwest on the Mitchell Lake Road Spur (14B) to the sign-marked junction with the South St. Vrain Trail (11). Go east on this 300 yards to the end of the wind swept clearing and turn north into the trees. A total skiing distance of 3.0 miles from Red Rock Trailhead (I).

USAGE

Nearly unused

SNOW CONDITIONS

Expect excellent snow conditions for the first part where the snow is protected by large trees, medium conditions for the steep bushwhack and poor to medium conditions for the mixed clearings and trees near timberline.

WIND EXPOSURE

Once the ridge is reached at 0.8 miles there is considerable wind exposure. Scattered clumps of trees provide some protection.

GRADIENT

Generally moderate but with a short steep climb from the boulder field up to the ridge at 0.8 miles and a steep descent from Point 10,894 into Beaver Creek.

ROUTE DESCRIPTION

From the east end of the 300 yard-long clearing near the western end of the South St. Vrain Trail (11), ski a compass course north northwest through large widely-spaced trees 900 yards to intersect an elongated clearing along the northern fork of South St. Vrain Creek (0.4 miles). Follow this clearing to its western end and then follow a 20 yard-wide tongue about 250 yards to the northwest on a gentle climb directly away from Niwot Mountain. The steep side of the glacial valley which must be climbed is visible ahead. Enter the trees and climb moderately steeply to a long, east-west boulder field across the slope where the slope steepens markedly. Move to the right (east) of the boulder field and climb the short steep section to the top of the ridge (0.8) miles. Keep as far west as possible to avoid the closely-spaced trees and large boulders further east.

Once the top is gained, head west along the ridge to the open meadow at 10,880 feet where there is a pronounced steepening of the ridge to the west and only scattered clumps of stunted trees above. The rocky above-timberline knoll just north-east of the junction of the Mt. Audubon trail with the Beaver Creek Trail (21) is visible on the skyline a half mile to the north. To the east of this knob is the rocky Point 10,964, lower and with low stunted trees. Contour north, along the base of the steeper slope to the west and at the edge of the trees, toward Point 10,964. Force a passage through the low trees at the top of the ridge into a 100 yard diameter clearing and the rock outcrop of Point 10,964 at 1.6 miles.

Descend the fall line north northwest through a series of four nearly-linked clearings in low trees to reach the mid-point at 10,760 feet of a 200 by 600 yard clearing on the main drainage of Beaver Creek. A narrow passage into the clearing through the thick low trees exists here at a minor step 90 yards above and southwest of a more prominent step near the lower end of the clearing. This is the 200 by 600 yard clearing at 2.7 miles on the Beaver Creek Trail (20). The Audubon Cutoff Route ends here.

ADDITIONAL CONNECTING TRAIL INFORMATION

None.

SPECIFIC SKILLS RECOMMENDED

Technical skiing
Advanced. The steep climb through thick trees on untracked snow to the ridge at 0.8 miles the above timberline conditions require advanced technique and equipment. The initial 0.6 miles are intermediate.

Endurance
Very strenuous. The requirements are nearly identical with those for the main Beaver Creek Trail (21).

Routefinding
Expert. The requirements are also nearly identical with those for the main Beaver Creek Trail.

VIEWS

Good views are to be had in all directions from Point 10,984. To the west is the summit of Mt. Audubon. To the north are Ogallala Peak, Elk Tooth, Mt. Copeland, the tips of Chiefs Head and Pagoda, Longs Peak, St. Vrain Mountain, Meadow Mountain, and the saddle on the Rock Creek Saddle Route (8B). To the east, the plains, Green Mountain, Nebelhorn, Sugarloaf, Bear Peak, and South Boulder Peak are visible. To the south are Niwot Mountain, the slopes above Left Hand Park Reservoir on the Niwot Ridge Traverse Route (19A), Mt. Albion, Kiowa and Arikaree Peaks.

PRIVATE PROPERTY AND OTHER RESTRICTIONS

The route is within the Indian Peaks Wilderness.

❄ ❄ ❄

TRAIL NO. 21B

FIREBREAK CUTOFF TRAIL

TRAIL MAPS: 8, 7

SUMMARY

This trail, when used along with the Four Wheel Drive Trail (10A), serves as an a link between the Coney Flats Trail (10) and the Beaver Creek Trail (21). The north end of the Beaver Creek Trail which is difficult to follow where there are only scattered trees is thereby bypassed. It can also serve as an emergency exit from the Beaver Creek Trail to Beaver Reservoir by going down the wide swath of the firebreak and continuing eastward on the easy terrain past Stapp Lakes. This should be used only in an emergency as the land is private and trespass is prohibited.

CLASSIFICATION: Difficult

MAPS (USGS 7.5' quadrangles)

Allens Park (A3)
Ward (B3)

ELEVATIONS (feet)

Starting....................................9360
Highest...................................10160
Cumulative gain 670
Cumulative loss..........................140

DISTANCE (miles, one way).......1.6

TIME (hours)

Outbound 1.4
Return 1.0

ACCESS

From the Beaver Reservoir North Trailhead (E), ski 1.3 miles west on the Coney Flats Trail (10) to the junction with the Four Wheel Drive Trail (10A). Turn left and ski southwest on it 0.4 miles to a switchback. A total distance of 1.7 miles.

USAGE

Nearly unused.

SNOW CONDITIONS

Medium.

WIND EXPOSURE

The 20 yard width of the swath through the trees results in the route being vulnerable to the effects of the wind.

GRADIENT

The moderate to steep gradient of this straight swath up the lower slopes of Mt. Audubon steepens slightly but uniformly with altitude.

ROUTE DESCRIPTION

From the switchback at 0.4 miles on the Four Wheel Drive Trail Alternate Trail (10A), continue south on a compass course without climbing. Intersect a rough bulldozed road which is followed southeast about 150 yards before leaving it to descend a short steep hillside to a large meadow at 0.6 miles. Cross to the west side of the clearing and pass two large concrete posts to enter the 20 yard wide firebreak cut through the dense forest on a straight line west.

The firebreak ends at 1.5 miles and 10,040 feet altitude in the bottom of a small tributary to Beaver Creek from the north. It is 200 yards west and 120 feet up to the Beaver Creek Trail. Careful attention to find the untracked trail is required. Once on it, it is generally easy to follow.

ADDITIONAL CONNECTING TRAIL INFORMATION

None.

SPECIFIC SKILLS RECOMMENDED

Technical skiing
Intermediate.

Endurance
Strenuous. The route will likely be untracked.

Routefinding
Advanced skills are necessary for finding the route from the switchback at the start of the route to where the actual firebreak begins.

VIEWS

Stapp Lake and Beaver Reservoir to the east. Mt. Audubon to the west.

PRIVATE PROPERTY AND OTHER RESTRICTIONS

Stapp Lake is privately owned and trespass is prohibited.

❄ ❄ ❄

PAWNEE PASS TRAIL

TRAIL MAP: 7

SUMMARY

A near twin to the Mitchell-Blue Lake Trail, access is by the same easy but well-used route that offers the comfort of a warming stop at the CMC Brainard Lake cabin. The routes diverge there, with the Pawnee Pass Trail continuing up the main valley of the South St. Vrain past Long Lake to Isabell Lake. Here, nestled in the deep valley at the base of Shoshoni Peak, the skiable route ends. A comparison of the two trails shows it to be shorter and climb less while staying on a more easily followed path through sheltering giant Engleman spruce.

CLASSIFICATION: Moderate-difficult.

MAPS (USGS 7.5' quadrangles)

Ward (B3)
Monarch Lake (B2)

ELEVATIONS (feet)

Starting..................................10500
Highest..................................10880
Cumulative gain 380
Cumulative loss............................0

DISTANCE (miles, one way).......1.9

TIME (hours)

Outbound 1.2
Return 0.9

ACCESS

From the Brainard Lake Trailhead (R), ski the Long Lake Road Spur (14C), 0.4 miles to the end at the summer parking lot. A total skiing distance of 3.0 miles from the Red Rock Trailhead (I).

USAGE

Light.

SNOW CONDITIONS

Excellent except in a few places that are exposed to the wind.

Long Lake outlet

WIND EXPOSURE

The trail generally stays in the protection of large trees but traverses a windy treeless slope as Lake Isabell is approached.

GRADIENT

The gradient is nearly flat except for a steep 150 feet climb near the end up the glacial step to Lake Isabell.

ROUTE DESCRIPTION

From the sign-marked trailhead at the Long Lake summer parking lot, ski west on the level blue diamond blazed trail 400 yards through dense trees to the east end of Long Lake. Here at a sign-marked junction, the Jean Lunning Trail (23) branches off to cross the dam. Here also is the wilderness boundary and the end of the blue diamond blazes.

Continue up the valley on the distinct trail through the large trees on the north side of first the lake and then of the meadow in the valley bottom. A sign marking a junction with the west end of the Jean Lunning Trail (23) is passed at 1.3 miles. Occasional wind-swept stretches where the edge of the meadow is skirted are encountered above here. The final 150 foot climb to Lake Isabell and the end of the described trail at 1.9 miles is surmounted by a pair of switchbacks in the trees and a short climb onto an open slope.

ADDITIONAL CONNECTING TRAIL INFORMATION

From the east end of Long Lake, the west end of the Long Lake Cutoff Trail

(24), is 100 yards to the south, across the dam.

SPECIFIC SKILLS RECOMMENDED

Technical skiing
Intermediate.

Endurance
Strenuous.

Routefinding
Beginner.

VIEWS

Open slopes near the shoreline of Isabell Lake offer dramatic views of the fine pyramid of Navajo Peak, Apache Peak, and the sheer east face of Shoshoni Peak.

PRIVATE PROPERTY AND OTHER RESTRICTIONS

The entire trail except the initial 0.2 miles is in the Indian Peaks Wilderness.

❄ ❄ ❄

TRAIL NO. 23

JEAN LUNNING TRAIL

TRAIL MAP: 7

SUMMARY

A near level, little-used trail with excellent and usually untracked snow. It parallels the Pawnee Pass Trail for over a mile, then crosses the open valley bottom with an unobstructed view of the east face of Shoshoni Peak to join it. Combined with the Pawnee Pass Trail, it makes a fine intermediate loop trip above Brainard Lake.

CLASSIFICATION: Moderate-difficult.

MAPS (USGS 7.5' quadrangles)

Ward (B3)
Monarch Lake (B2)

ELEVATIONS (feet)

Starting....................................10520
Highest.....................................10650
Cumulative gain 130
Cumulative loss...........................40

DISTANCE (miles, one way).......1.5

TIME (hours)

Outbound 0.9
Return 0.9

ACCESS

From the Brainard Lake Trailhead (R), ski west on the Long Lake Road Spur (14C) 0.4 miles to its end at the summer parking lot. From here, ski west on the Pawnee Pass Trail (22), 0.4 miles to the sign-marked junction at the north end of the dam on the eastern shore of Long Lake. A total skiing distance from Red Rock Trailhead (I), of 3.4 miles.

An alternate access route from Brainard Lake is the Long Lake Cutoff Trail (24) which ends at the south end of the dam.

USAGE

Very light.

SNOW CONDITIONS

Excellent, probably untracked. The area near the dam may be poor due to wind.

WIND EXPOSURE

Although very exposed to wind at the dam, and exposed to a lesser degree at the meadow crossing at the upper end, the trail is in trees and well protected for most of the route.

GRADIENT

Nearly flat.

Shoshoni Peak from Jean Lunning Trail

ROUTE DESCRIPTION

Cross to the south side of the dam and the sign-marked junction with the Long Lake Cutoff Trail (24). Ski southwest into the large trees to find the trail which parallels the lake shore at a distance of about 100 yards. The unblazed trail can be difficult to follow exactly if untracked, watch for the footbridge railings at gully crossings.

Continue up valley in the trees about a half mile past the end of the lake before crossing the valley bottom to a footbridge on the creek at 1.4 miles and on to the junction in the trees on the north side with the Pawnee Pass Trail (22) at 1.5

miles.

ADDITIONAL CONNECTING TRAIL INFORMATION

This trail forks off at mile 0.4 on the Pawnee Pass Trail (22) and rejoins it at mile 1.3.

SPECIFIC SKILLS RECOMMENDED

Technical skiing
Novice.

Endurance
Moderate.

Routefinding
Intermediate.

VIEWS

Apache and Shoshoni Peaks are visible at the head of the valley from the footbridge crossed at 1.4 miles.

PRIVATE PROPERTY AND OTHER RESTRICTIONS

The entire trail is within the Indian Peaks Wilderness.

❄ ❄ ❄

TRAIL NO. 24

LONG LAKE CUTOFF TRAIL

TRAIL MAP: 7

SUMMARY

A shortcut from Brainard Lake to Long Lake and the Jean Lunning and Pawnee Pass Trails, it generally offers excellent snow, frequently untracked, for the first half of its course. Passage into the second half, an open area more subject to wind, is marked by a roadcut frequently offering a choice of a rocky roadbed or a dense thicket. In addition to being shorter, it is of more interest than the alternative Long Lake Road Spur.

CLASSIFICATION: Moderate.

MAPS (USGS 7.5' quadrangles)

Ward (B3)

ELEVATIONS (feet)

Starting...................................10360

Highest.....................................10530
Cumulative gain 170
Cumulative loss...........................0

DISTANCE (miles, one way).......0.5

TIME (hours)

Outbound 0.4
Return 0.3

ACCESS

At the Brainard Lake Trailhead (R), go to the sign-marked junction at the southwest corner of the Brainard Lake Loop Road (14A). The trail sign is on top of a road-cut opposite an outdoor toilet. A total skiing distance from Red Rock Trailhead (I), of 2.4 miles.

USAGE

Very light.

SNOW CONDITIONS

Excellent in the protection of large trees for the eastern half, but poor in the wind-swept open areas to the west.

WIND EXPOSURE

Protected by large trees in the east, more exposed in the west where the force of the wind is broken only by scattered clumps of trees.

GRADIENT

Moderate in the east, slight to moderate in the west.

ROUTE DESCRIPTION

From the sign-marked junction on the Brainard Lake Road Loop, ski west on the unblazed trail through moderately spaced large trees as it climbs 120 feet through four switchbacks at intervals of 60 to 120 yards. Proceed west through a wind-scoured area of meadow and scattered stunted trees, staying near the boundary of the gentle valley bottom and the steep tree-covered slope. The sign-marked junction with the Jean Lunning Trail (23) is in an open meadow at the east end of Long Lake at 0.5 miles.

ADDITIONAL CONNECTING TRAIL INFORMATION

The Pawnee Pass Trail (22) is across the dam, 100 yards north of the western end of the trail.

SPECIFIC SKILLS RECOMMENDED

Technical skiing
Beginner.

Endurance
Moderate.

Routefinding
Intermediate.

VIEWS

Apache and Shoshoni Peaks are visible from the open areas at the western end.

PRIVATE PROPERTY AND OTHER RESTRICTIONS

None.

❁ ❁ ❁

TRAIL NO. 25

RAINBOW LAKES ROAD

TRAIL MAPS: 11, 10

SUMMARY

Memories of the bustle of summer activity contrasts with the quiet serenity of snowdrifts on picnic tables at the Rainbow Lakes Campground. Reached by skiing the four miles of unplowed road from the Mountain Research Station Trailhead that may at places be blown clear, it can serve as a destination itself, or be the starting point for the more challenging Glacier Rim Route.

CLASSIFICATION: Moderate.

MAPS (USGS 7.5' quadrangles)

Ward (B3)

ELEVATIONS (feet)

Starting....................................9290
Highest....................../......................9960
Cumulative gain 740
Cumulative loss...........................70

DISTANCE (miles, one way).......4.0

TIME (hours)

Outbound 2.0
Return 1.5

ACCESS

At the Mountain Research Station Trailhead (J)

USAGE

Very light.

SNOW CONDITIONS

Very poor unless skied after a snowfall. Road corners exposed to sun and wind can be rocky.

WIND EXPOSURE

Exposure to wind is significant for westward travel.

GRADIENT

The gradient ranges from nearly flat to slight. Some sections of only slight gradient however, are long and with a hard packed surface can provide a rapid return.

ROUTE DESCRIPTION

From the roadside parking at the Mountain Research Station Trailhead (J), the obvious wide road follows a curving, generally climbing course to the southwest. Pass a log arch at 1.0 miles, the locked gate to the City of Boulder watershed at 2.5 miles, and continue past the picnic tables, outhouses, and signs of the Rainbow Lakes Campground to the summer trailhead signs for the Glacier Rim and Rainbow Lakes trails at 4.0 miles.

ADDITIONAL CONNECTING TRAIL INFORMATION

The Caribou Creek Trail (27) branches off to the left (south) at 3.3 miles onto a jeep road marked with a sign *Forest Service Road 505.*

The Glacier Rim Trail (26) continues to the north from a summer trailhead sign at the end of this trail.

The Rainbow Lakes Bowl Route (26A) continues west from the end of this trail.

SPECIFIC SKILLS RECOMMENDED

Technical skiing
Only novice skills are required to ski this wide road of slight gradient given medium snow conditions.

Endurance
Moderate to ski the entire distance.

Routefinding
Novice skills are adequate to follow this wide road. It can readily be followed in darkness or reduced visibility due to blowing snow.

VIEWS

At 2.2 miles the road rounds a small knoll where views of the east shoulder of Arapaho Ridge, Arapaho Peak, Mt. Albion, Kiowa Peak, and Niwot Ridge are revealed.

PRIVATE PROPERTY AND OTHER RESTRICTIONS

The prohibited area of the City of Boulder watershed is well marked at a locked gate at 2.5 miles.

❊ ❊ ❊

TRAIL NO. 26

GLACIER RIM TRAIL

TRAIL MAP: 10

SUMMARY

A seldom traveled forest trail from Rainbow Lakes Campground leads to a timberline overlook of the headwaters of North Boulder Creek and views up the valley to North Arapaho Peak and Arapaho Glacier. The price of admission is the long ski-in on the Rainbow Lakes Road. An attractive alternative return to the campground descends the open slopes of the Rainbow Lakes Bowl Route.

CLASSIFICATION: Difficult.

MAPS (USGS 7.5' quadrangles)

Ward (B3)

ELEVATIONS (feet)

Starting.....................................9960
Highest.....................................11030
Cumulative gain.......................1070
Cumulative loss............................0

DISTANCE (miles, one way).......1.9

TIME (hours)

Outbound.....................................1.8
Return...1.0

ACCESS

From Mountain Research Station Trailhead (J), ski the Rainbow Lakes Road (25) 4.0 miles to the end at Rainbow Lakes Campground.

USAGE

Nearly unused.

SNOW CONDITIONS

Excellent

WIND EXPOSURE

The trail is well protected until it emerges from the trees at a timberline overlook near the end of the trail.

GRADIENT

Moderate, with the last 500 vertical feet the steepest.

ROUTE DESCRIPTION

From the sign-marked trailhead at the west end of the Rainbow Lakes Campground area, the unblazed but easy to follow trail climbs to the north. It soon encounters and follows the City of Boulder watershed barbwire fence and signs to 10,530 feet where it switchbacks to the left at a larger *No Trespassing* sign. The trail then stays on the south side of the definite ridge. A group of four switchbacks at 10,660 and a pair at 10,860 are not shown on the USGS topographic map. The last section of trail becomes difficult to follow and is lost as it emerges from the trees near the ridge crest at 11,000 feet.

ADDITIONAL CONNECTING TRAIL INFORMATION

The west or upper end of the trail connects with the Rainbow Lakes Bowl Route (26A), an alternate return route to Rainbow Lakes Campground.

SPECIFIC SKILLS RECOMMENDED

Technical skiing
Intermediate, a return by this route is less difficult than the optional return by the Rainbow Lakes Bowl Route.

Endurance
Very strenuous, this trail has to be combined with the long access route.

Routefinding
Intermediate, routefinding on this generally untracked trail becomes increasingly difficult with distance and altitude.

VIEWS

There is little to see until the trail emerges from the trees near the end. Mt. Albion, Arikaree and Kiowa Peaks then come into view across the southern fork of North Boulder Creek. The lakes of the City of Boulder's forbidden watershed; Triple Lakes, Goose, Island, and Silver Lakes are immediately below. North Arapaho Peak and Arapaho Glacier make a splendid view at the head of the valley to the west.

The permanent snowfield on the eastern end of Arapaho Ridge, so prominent as to be readily visible from Boulder, is visible to the southwest and the pediment surface of the eastern slope of the Front Range is to the south and east.

PRIVATE PROPERTY AND OTHER RESTRICTIONS

Trespass into the City of Boulder watershed immediately to the north is prohibited.

❀ ❀ ❀

TRAIL NO. 26A

RAINBOW LAKES BOWL ROUTE

TRAIL MAP: 10

SUMMARY

An alternate return route from the Glacier Rim Trail, this off-trail route descends open slopes 650 feet to more gentle wooded terrain. Bushwhacking down the drainage then provides a return to the Rainbow Lakes Campground.

CLASSIFICATION: Difficult.

MAPS (USGS 7.5' quadrangles)

Ward (B3)

ELEVATIONS (feet)

Starting....................................11030
Highest.....................................11030
Cumulative gain 0
Cumulative loss......................1070

DISTANCE (miles, one way).......1.9

TIME (hours)

Outbound (ascent) 2.0
Return (descent) 1.7

ACCESS

Access to the upper end or most common starting point, is to ski from the Mountain Research Station Trailhead (J), 4.0 miles on the Rainbow Lakes Road (25) to its end at Rainbow Lakes Campground. From here, ski 1.9 miles on the Glacier Rim Trail (26), 1.9 miles to its end. A total distance of 5.9 miles.

Access to the lower end is at the Rainbow Lakes Campground.

USAGE

Nearly unused.

SNOW CONDITIONS

Good in the shelter of the trees, medium on the open slopes of the bowl where it can be hard wind slab, and also only medium where exposed along the Rainbow Lakes.

WIND EXPOSURE

Very exposed on the descent of the open bowl and again along the lakes.

GRADIENT

The gradient of the bowl is steep, descending 650 feet in a half mile.

ROUTE DESCRIPTION

From the high point of the Glacier Rim Trail, descend south to the bowl, and then east southeast down the treeless slopes to the flat clearing. Head south a quarter mile down the drainage through thick trees to intercept the summer trail or continue down the drainage as it turns east and bushwhack to Rainbow Lakes Campground.

ADDITIONAL CONNECTING TRAIL INFORMATION

None.

SPECIFIC SKILLS RECOMMENDED

Technical skiing
Expert, hard windslab can be encountered in the bowl.

Endurance
Very strenuous when combined with the access trails.

Routefinding
Advanced skills are required as most of the route follows no recognizable features other than drainage.

VIEWS

None other than those at the high end which are listed for the Glacier Rim Trail.

PRIVATE PROPERTY AND OTHER RESTRICTIONS

None.

❄ ❄ ❄

TRAIL NO. 27

CARIBOU CREEK TRAIL

TRAIL MAPS: 11, 10, 13

SUMMARY

Despite its high altitude this trail doesn't have the tree cover to give adequate protection for consistently good snow. Along with the Caribou Flat Route, it links the trails of the Brainard Lake area with those of Eldora. Perhaps the major reason for skiing it may be the challenge of doing just that.

CLASSIFICATION: Moderate.

MAPS (USGS 7.5' quadrangles)

Ward (B3)
Nederland (C3)

ELEVATIONS (feet)

Starting....................................9990
Highest....................................9990
Cumulative gain 120
Cumulative loss........................290

DISTANCE (miles, one way).......2.3

TIME (hours)

Outbound (southbound) 1.1
Return (northbound)...................1.1

ACCESS

North end. From the Mountain Research Station Trailhead (J), ski the Rainbow Lakes Road (25) 3.3 miles to a jeep road branching off to the left and marked with a sign *Forest Service Road 505.*

South end. At the Caribou Trailhead (K).

USAGE

Nearly unused.

SNOW CONDITIONS

Very poor, the southern part, where the jeep road route is more sheltered by trees, is better.

WIND EXPOSURE

Moderate due to lack of sheltering trees.

GRADIENT

Nearly flat.

ROUTE DESCRIPTION

From the junction at 3.3 miles on the Rainbow Lakes Road (25), ski south on Forest Service Road 505 as it descends toward Caribou Creek. At 130 yards, take the less prominent fork to the right and descend to the creek on an easy route.

Ski up the broad gentle valley, crossing to the east side at Pomeroy Mountain where a jeep road is generally in the shelter of trees and better protected than is the open brushy bottom of Caribou Park. The road climbs on a gentle grade past a winter closure gate, and 170 yards more to the saddle and the Caribou Trailhead (K) at 2.3 miles.

ADDITIONAL CONNECTING TRAIL INFORMATION

The left fork at 130 yards continues 700 yards more to dead-end at an overlook of the creek.

The south end joins the Caribou Flat Route (28) at the Caribou Trailhead (K).

SPECIFIC SKILLS RECOMMENDED

Technical skiing
Novice.

Endurance
Moderate.

Routefinding
Beginner.

VIEWS

The mass of the Arapaho Peaks dominates the skyline to the northwest.

PRIVATE PROPERTY AND OTHER RESTRICTIONS

Private mining operations are in the area. The road to the Caribou Trailhead is plowed by local mining operators and should not be totally relied on.

❄ ❄ ❄

TRAIL NO. 28

CARIBOU FLAT ROUTE

TRAIL MAP: 13

SUMMARY

Along with the Caribou Creek Trail, Rainbow Lakes Road, and Sourdough, South Trail it links the trails of Brainard Lake to Eldora. The south end of this unblazed and untracked route is at the Fourth of July Road in the valley bottom of the North Fork of Middle Boulder Creek. From here it climbs steeply a gruelling thousand feet through dense small trees onto Caribou Flat. The remainder of the route follows a jeep road over easy terrain but generally poor snow to a trailhead at the ghost town of Caribou.

CLASSIFICATION: Difficult.

MAPS (USGS 7.5' quadrangles)

Nederland (C3)

ELEVATIONS (feet)

```
Starting....................................9320
Highest....................................10330
Cumulative gain ......................1010
Cumulative loss.........................330
```

DISTANCE (miles, one way).......2.6

TIME (hours)

```
Outbound (northbound)...............2.2
Return (southbound)...................1.7
```

ACCESS

South end. From the Eldora Trailhead (L), ski west on the King Lake Trail (29) 0.8 miles, then 0.9 miles north up the Fourth of July Road (32) to an unmarked turn off at 9,370 feet altitude. The road makes a slight turn to the left here at the crest of a long moderate climb through an aspen bordered clearing. Total distance 1.7 miles.

North end. At Caribou Trailhead (K).

USAGE

Nearly unused.

SNOW CONDITIONS

Poor overall. A variety of snow conditions will probably be encountered with deep unconsolidated snow in the small dense trees on the climb out of the valley, wind slab at the ridge, and thin snow on Caribou Flat due to the lack of tree cover.

WIND EXPOSURE

A major portion of the route, on Caribou Flat and on the ridge south of Point 10,335, lacks adequate tree cover to provide wind protection.

GRADIENT

The southern part of the route on the climb out of the valley and up the ridge up to Point 10,334 is steep to very steep. The remainder of the route is nearly flat.

ROUTE DESCRIPTION

Turn off the Fourth of July Road (32) to the right at 0.9 miles and 9370 feet altitude, where the road makes a slight turn to the left and climb moderately steeply through large, well separated trees on a traverse to the left to 9,500 feet. Switchback right and climb steeply through dense small trees, passing below a boulder field, and up a ramp to the ridge at 0.7 miles and 10,040 feet. Climb a steep treeless section up the ridge and continue through scattered trees to the summit of Point 10,335 at 1.1 miles.

Descend slightly through low trees to the jeep road and follow it north across the nearly level Caribou Flat where signs warning of the dangers of abandoned mines in the area help mark the path of the road. The road descends northeast across the east side of Caribou Hill, past an abandoned cabin to the saddle and the Caribou Trailhead (K) at 2.6 miles.

In skiing the route from north to south in poor visibility, be wary of following the indistinct jeep road where one fork can mistakenly be followed west toward Klondike Mountain. This can be avoided by climbing only to 10,220 feet and then following a compass course south without climbing.

ADDITIONAL CONNECTING TRAIL INFORMATION

None

SPECIFIC SKILLS RECOMMENDED

Technical skiing
Advanced level skill is recommended for the ridge south of Point 10,335.

Endurance
Very strenuous because of the steep, thousand foot ascent or descent through

dense small trees on an untracked route.

Routefinding
Advanced.

VIEWS

From the ridge south from Point 10,335, a panorama of peaks and valleys can be seen in all directions. To the north from left to right, are Arapaho Peak, Klondike Mountain, Bald Mountain, Arapaho Ridge with the snow bowl above Rainbow Lakes, Caribou Hill, and the saddle at Caribou townsite at the north end of this trail.

To the south, James Peak rises above Bryan Mountain and the Eldora ski runs. The North Gully of Bryan Mountain Route (34), the windswept slopes of Bryan Mountain, and the mine cabin above Lost Lake are visible. Beyond are Mt. Thorodin, the north facing slopes of the bowl above the Jenny Lind Gulch Trail (38), and Mt. Evans.

To the west is Guinn Mountain, Rollins Pass, the trestles of the Moffat Railroad high above the valley of the South Fork of Middle Boulder Creek, and the King Lake Trail (29) in the valley bottom.

PRIVATE PROPERTY AND OTHER RESTRICTIONS

Stay on the jeep road to avoid mine workings or other private property.

❄ ❄ ❄

TRAIL NO. 29

KING LAKE TRAIL

TRAIL MAPS: 13, 12

SUMMARY

Starting at the town of Eldora, the trail follows the valley bottom of the South Fork of Boulder Creek upstream to close under Rollins Pass at the continental divide. The trail is initially a well used unplowed road, but as trails branch off to go up tributary valleys, it becomes a trail and eventually changes to an untracked route when if becomes impossible to distinguish the summer trail.

CLASSIFICATION: Difficult, due mainly to the length.

MAPS (USGS 7.5' quadrangles)

Nederland (C3)
East Portal (C4)

ELEVATIONS (feet)

Starting.................................8810

Highest 10900
Cumulative gain 2090
Cumulative loss............................0

DISTANCE (miles, one way).......3.8

TIME (hours)

Outbound 3.8
Return 2.3

Moffat Road trestles above King Lake Trail

ACCESS

At Eldora Town Trailhead (L).

USAGE

Very light, although this grades from heavy at the beginning to nearly unused at the upper end.

SNOW CONDITIONS

Excellent at the upper end and overall, but poor at the beginning.

WIND EXPOSURE

Generally well protected by trees, there are a few exposed areas in the first part.

GRADIENT

Moderate gradients are above Hessie and above the confluence with Jasper Creek. Most of the remainder is a slight but steady climb.

ROUTE DESCRIPTION

Ski the unplowed road west from Eldora past the turn-off of the Fourth of July Road (32) at 0.8 miles. Follow the left fork with the *Hessie Road* sign past cabins at the site of Hessie at 1.1 miles. Continue to the summer trailhead at a crossing of the North Fork of Middle Boulder Creek at 1.3 miles.

After switchbacking to climb a steep treeless slope, the road levels out before reaching a vehicle bridge over the South Fork of Middle Boulder Creek at 2.3 miles. A sign here shows the Devils Thumb Trail to branch off to the right onto a steep narrow summer hiking trail. The road is the better choice even if Devil's Thumb Trail is one's goal. A junction with it is reached later at 2.8 miles.
From the bridge, continue up the wind scoured road to the crest of a moderate climb and a sign-marked junction with the Lost Lake Trail (33) at 2.6 miles. Proceed another 400 yards along the flat valley bottom to a sign-marked junction with the Devils Thumb Trail (30) at 2.8 miles in a wide level open area at the confluence of Jasper Creek, on the right, and the South Fork of Middle Boulder Creek, straight ahead.

The distinct trail climbs through trees up a moderate slope, past the last two blue diamond blazes and enters the Indian Peaks Wilderness. The now unblazed trail can be followed only for about a mile, up the north side of the valley of the South Fork, until it becomes too indistinct to follow.

Beyond here the route goes well either on the north side or in the creek bed. As you pass below the railroad trestles the valley floor widens and it is possible to ski either side. End the tour at a clearing at 10,900 feet and 6.1 miles. The steep slopes at the end of the valley may present an avalanche hazard for travel beyond here.

ADDITIONAL CONNECTING TRAIL INFORMATION

An unmarked junction with the Lower Gully Bryan Mountain Route (34A) is at 1.5 miles.

SPECIFIC SKILLS RECOMMENDED

Technical skiing
Beginner.

Endurance
Very strenuous.

Routefinding
Intermediate.

VIEWS

Devils Thumb on the continental divide may be seen up the valley of Jasper Creek from near the junction with the Lost Lake Trail at 2.6 miles.

The railroad trestles, high above on the south valley wall, are visible from the upper part of the trail, as is the corniced ridge on the continental divide at the head of the valley.

PRIVATE PROPERTY AND OTHER RESTRICTIONS

Posted private property is along the roadway at the lower end and cabins and property at Hessie are privately owned. The trail beyond the junction with the Devils Thumb Trail at 2.8 miles is within the Indian Peaks Wilderness.

❄ ❄ ❄

TRAIL NO. 30

DEVILS THUMB ROUTE

TRAIL MAPS: 13, 12

SUMMARY

One of the most spectacular and exhilarating powder ski runs described in this book, it follows one of the tributary valleys to Middle Boulder Creek above Eldora. Starting as a jeep road in the wide gentle valley, it changes to a trail which soon becomes unrecognizable and one picks a route through widely spaced trees to climb to the bench of Jasper Lake and then over open rolling terrain above timberline to Devils Thumb Lake.

CLASSIFICATION: Very difficult.

MAPS (USGS 7.5' quadrangles)

Nederland (C3)
East Portal (C2)

ELEVATIONS (feet)

Starting.................................9620
Highest.................................11280
Cumulative gain.......................1660
Cumulative loss............................0

DISTANCE (miles, one way).......4.2

TIME (hours)

Outbound..................................3.6
Return...2.0

ACCESS

From the Eldora Town Trailhead (L), ski west on the King Lake Trail (29), 2.8 miles to a sign-marked junction.

USAGE

Very light.

SNOW CONDITIONS

Excellent.

WIND EXPOSURE

Only moderate, much of the route is not protected by dense trees but the snow pack does not exhibit much wind effect.

GRADIENT

Moderate with locally steep sections.

Toward Devils Thumb

ROUTE DESCRIPTION

From the sign-marked junction on the King Lake Trail (29), follow the jeep road along the west side of the broad flat-bottomed valley past a wilderness boundary sign in 300 yards and a sign-marked junction with the Woodland Lake Trail (31) at 0.9 miles.

Beyond this junction, the jeep road crosses the creek and as the trees thin out, climbs more steeply along the north valley wall and onto the crest of a small medial ridge in the valley bottom. It then descends slightly to the right to become unidentifiable. Climb to the west along the north side of the valley, switchbacking where necessary to gain the bench and Jasper Lake at 10,814 feet and 3.1 miles. Continue west without climbing significantly to the open slopes east of Devils Thumb Lake, then climb 500 feet past the lake to the top of the 11,280 foot knoll 200 yards south of the lake and the end of the tour at 4.2 miles.

ADDITIONAL CONNECTING TRAIL INFORMATION

The upper end of the route joins the Jasper Creek Route (30A), an alternate descent route.

SPECIFIC SKILLS RECOMMENDED

Technical skiing
Expert.

Endurance
Very strenuous.

Routefinding
Advanced.

VIEWS

The knoll at the end of the tour gives unobstructed views of the corniced ridge of the continental divide and of the rock spire of Devils Thumb, both only a half mile distant.

PRIVATE PROPERTY AND OTHER RESTRICTIONS

Almost all of the route is within the Indian Peaks Wilderness.

❊ ❊ ❊

Near Jasper Lake

TRAIL NO. 30A

JASPER CREEK ROUTE

TRAIL MAP: 12

SUMMARY

An alternate to the upper part of the Devils Thumb Route, the moderate treeless slopes at the upper end provide superb telemarking on the descent to the valley bottom where a gentle route through tall trees can be followed a mile before contouring out to rejoin the Devils Thumb Route.

CLASSIFICATION: Very difficult.

MAPS (USGS 7.5' quadrangles)

East Portal (C2)

ELEVATIONS (feet)

Starting 11280
Highest 11280
Cumulative gain 0
Cumulative loss.........................990

DISTANCE (miles, one way).......2.2

TIME (hours)

Outbound (uphill) 1.7
Return (downhill)........................0.8

ACCESS

West end. From the Eldora Trailhead (L), ski west on the King Lake Trail (29), 2.8 miles to the Devils Thumb Route (30), and 4.2 miles on it to its end on the 11,280 foot knoll south of Devils Thumb. A total distance of 7.0 miles from the Eldora Trailhead.

East end. At mile 2.8 on the Devils Thumb Route. This is on a small medial ridge at 10,300 feet and is 4.9 miles from Eldora Trailhead.

USAGE

Very light.

SNOW CONDITIONS

Excellent.

WIND EXPOSURE

Moderate, the west end is unprotected by trees but the snow shows little effect from the wind.

Approaching Devils Thumb

GRADIENT

Steep at the west end, nearly flat in the valley bottom.

ROUTE DESCRIPTION

Descend the steep treeless slopes south from the 11,280 foot knoll south of Devils Thumb Lake into the tall trees of the Jasper Creek drainage. Continue east along the bottom as the slope lessens and contour out to the north at 10,300 feet to join the Devils Thumb Route (30). Avoid the steep section lower on the creek.

ADDITIONAL CONNECTING TRAIL INFORMATION

Both ends of this alternate route connect with the Devils Thumb Route (30).

SPECIFIC SKILLS RECOMMENDED

Technical skiing
Expert.

Endurance
Very strenuous.

Routefinding
Advanced.

Devils Thumb Pass

129

VIEWS

The best views of the corniced ridge of the continental divide and Devils Thumb are from the knoll at the west end. These are identical with those described for the Devils Thumb Route.

PRIVATE PROPERTY AND OTHER RESTRICTIONS

The entire route is within the Indian Peaks Wilderness.

❄ ❄ ❄

TRAIL NO. 31

WOODLAND LAKE TRAIL

TRAIL MAP: 12

SUMMARY

A steep climb up a tributary valley to Middle Boulder Creek above Eldora leads to a timberline lake set in a glacial cirque. Much of the way is not on a recognizable trail. The deep powder snow amongst the large trees on the steep lower section gives way to wind sculptured snow and stunted trees as the lake is approached.

CLASSIFICATION: Very difficult.

MAPS (USGS 7.5' quadrangles)

East Portal (C2)

ELEVATIONS (feet)

Starting.....................................9710
Highest...................................10980
Cumulative gain 1270
Cumulative loss.............................0

DISTANCE (miles, one way).......1.9

TIME (hours)

Outbound 1.7
Return 1.2

ACCESS

From the Eldora Town Trailhead (L), ski west on the King Lake Trail (29), 2.8 miles to the Devils Thumb Route (30), and 0.9 miles up it to a sign-marked junction. A total distance of 3.7 miles.

USAGE

Nearly unused.

SNOW CONDITIONS

Good overall, excellent in the trees but only medium on the open slope entering the drainage and in the wind swept area near the lake.

WIND EXPOSURE

Exposed to high winds east of the lake.

GRADIENT

Moderate overall with steep sections and a very steep section above the cabins at 0.5 miles.

ROUTE DESCRIPTION

From the sign-marked junction on the Devils Thumb Route (30), ski west up a jeep road as it climbs high on the south side of Woodland Creek. At 0.4 miles the road crosses the creek where two old cabins are visible 200 yards ahead. Beyond here, the road is no longer identifiable. Climb about 300 feet up the steep open slopes beyond the cabins and move left into the trees and a minor gully where the opportunity is offered. As the slope lessens, move left toward the streambed in the relatively widely spaced groups of trees and open windswept areas until the lake is reached at 1.9 miles.

ADDITIONAL CONNECTING TRAIL INFORMATION

The route may be continued beyond Woodland Lake on the Woodland Mountain Overlook Route (31A).

SPECIFIC SKILLS RECOMMENDED

Technical skiing
Expert.

Endurance
Strenuous.

Routefinding
Advanced.

VIEWS

The spectacular glacial cirque setting of Woodland Lake and Skyscraper Reservoir is visible ahead through the stunted trees near the lake.

PRIVATE PROPERTY AND OTHER RESTRICTIONS

The entire trail is within the Indian Peaks Wilderness.

TRAIL NO. 31A

WOODLAND MOUNTAIN OVERLOOK ROUTE

TRAIL MAP: 12

SUMMARY

A short bushwhacking climb through the tall trees from Woodland Lake south to the ridgetop gives an unique view of Rollins Pass and the railroad trestles above the valley of the South Fork of Middle Boulder Creek.

CLASSIFICATION: Very difficult.

MAPS (USGS 7.5' quadrangles)

East Portal (C2)

ELEVATIONS (feet)

Starting..................................10980
Highest..................................11260
Cumulative gain 280
Cumulative loss.............................0

DISTANCE (miles, one way).......0.3

Moffat Road trestles from Wonderland Mountain

TIME (hours)

Outbound 0.5
Return 0.3

ACCESS

From the Eldora Trailhead (L), ski west on the King Lake Trail (29) 2.8 miles to the Devils Thumb Route (30), 0.9 miles on it to the Woodland Lake Trail (31), and 1.9 miles up it to its end at Woodland Lake. A total distance of 5.6 miles.

USAGE

Nearly unused.

SNOW CONDITIONS

Excellent.

WIND EXPOSURE

Very little.

GRADIENT

Very steep.

ROUTE DESCRIPTION

Pick a route south from the lake 300 feet up through deep untracked powder snow between the widely spaced tall trees to the ridgetop at 0.3 miles.

ADDITIONAL CONNECTING TRAIL INFORMATION

A descent south from the ridgetop into the South Fork of Middle Boulder Creek to the King Lake Trail (29) should not be attempted if unstable snow conditions exist.

SPECIFIC SKILLS RECOMMENDED

Technical skiing
Expert.

Endurance
Strenuous.

Routefinding
Advanced.

VIEWS

The view across the South Fork of Middle Boulder Creek to the railroad trestles and Rollins Pass is spectacular.

PRIVATE PROPERTY AND OTHER RESTRICTIONS

The entire route is within the Indian Peaks Wilderness.

❄ ❄ ❄

TRAIL NO. 32

FOURTH OF JULY ROAD

TRAIL MAPS: 13, 12

SUMMARY

A long but easy tour follows the road up the straight glacial trough of the valley of the North Fork of Middle Boulder Creek above Eldora. The road ends at the City of Boulder's Buckingham Campground at the base of Arapaho Pass.

CLASSIFICATION: Moderate-difficult.

MAPS (USGS 7.5' quadrangles)

East Portal (C2)
Nederland (C3)
Monarch Lake (B2)

ELEVATIONS (feet)

Starting....................................8990
Highest...................................10160
Cumulative gain.......................1170
Cumulative loss.............................0

DISTANCE (miles, one way).......4.3

TIME (hours)

Outbound 2.5
Return 1.7

ACCESS

From the Eldora Trailhead (L), ski west on the King Lake Trail (29), 0.5 miles to a sign-marked junction.

USAGE

Moderate at the bottom, decreasing to light at the top.

SNOW CONDITIONS

Medium overall. Poor and frequently icy for the first 0.7 mile on a south facing slope which has the steepest gradient of the trip. Snow conditions improve to medium to good thereafter, but are affected by wind near the end.

WIND EXPOSURE

The road becomes increasingly exposed to the wind in the final mile.

GRADIENT

Moderate for the first 0.7 mile, slight thereafter.

ROUTE DESCRIPTION

The unplowed passenger car road is followed up the bottom of the valley to Buckingham Campground and continues 200 yards in the shelter of trees to a gate and sign marking the boundary of private property at 4.2 miles.

ADDITIONAL CONNECTING TRAIL INFORMATION

A junction with the unmarked Caribou Flat Route (28), is at 0.9 miles, where the road makes a slight turn to the left at the crest of a long easy climb through an aspen bordered clearing.

SPECIFIC SKILLS RECOMMENDED

Technical skiing
Beginner.

Endurance
Moderate.

Routefinding
Novice.

VIEWS

Arapaho Pass and South Arapaho Peak tower ahead for most of the trip. Mt. Neva and unnamed glaciated peaks are visible to the left from near Buckingham Campground.

PRIVATE PROPERTY AND OTHER RESTRICTIONS

Numerous private cabins crowd the roadway for most of its length. Passage up the bottom of the valley beyond Buckingham Campground is blocked by private land.

❄ ❄ ❄

TRAIL NO. 33

LOST LAKE TRAIL

TRAIL MAP: 13

SUMMARY

A short easy climb off the King Lake Trail west of Eldora leads to this secluded lake nestled on a bench on the steep north slopes of Bryan Mountain.

CLASSIFICATION: Moderate.

MAPS (USGS 7.5' quadrangles)

Nederland (C3)

ELEVATIONS (feet)

```
Starting..................................9620
Highest...................................9780
Cumulative gain .........................160
Cumulative loss..............................0
```

DISTANCE (miles, one way).......0.5

TIME (hours)

```
Outbound ...................................0.5
Return ........................................0.3
```

ACCESS

From the Eldora Trailhead (L), ski west on the King Lake Trail (29), 2.6 miles to a sign-marked junction at the top of a moderate climb.

USAGE

Very light.

SNOW CONDITIONS

Medium.

WIND EXPOSURE

Exposed to wind at a brushy meadow about midway along the trail.

GRADIENT

Slight.

ROUTE DESCRIPTION

From the sign-marked junction with the King Lake Trail (29), follow the easy, well-defined but unblazed trail, as it climbs through trees up the drainage below Lost Lake. Take the right of two forks where the left can be seen to cross the drainage on a footbridge with a handrail. The trail becomes difficult to recognize as it curves to the west through a brushy meadow but reappears in the trees at the west end. Here it curves back east and climbs to Lost Lake at 0.5 miles.

ADDITIONAL CONNECTING TRAIL INFORMATION

The North Gully of Bryan Mountain Route (34), and Lower Gully Route (34A) both connect with the end of the trail at Lost Lake.

SPECIFIC SKILLS RECOMMENDED

Technical skiing
Beginner.

Endurance
Easy.

Routefinding
Beginner.

VIEWS

An abandoned mine building is visible high above the lake on the precipitous scree slopes of Bryan Mountain. Chittenden Mountain is visible to the north across Middle Boulder Creek.

PRIVATE PROPERTY AND OTHER RESTRICTIONS

None.

❄ ❄ ❄

TRAIL NO. 34

NORTH GULLY BRYAN MOUNTAIN ROUTE

TRAIL MAPS: 13, 12

SUMMARY

The trails of Middle Boulder Creek west of Eldora are joined with those above Eldora Ski Area and Jenny Creek by this connecting route that ascends a very steep gully and then follows the natural gas pipeline swath along the ridge top to Arestua Hut.

CLASSIFICATION: Very difficult.

MAPS (USGS 7.5' quadrangles)

Nederland (C3)
East Portal (C2)

ELEVATIONS (feet)

Starting.....................................9780
Highest....................................10960
Cumulative gain 1240
Cumulative loss............................60

DISTANCE (miles, one way).......2.1

TIME (hours)

Outbound (uphill) 2.0
Return (downhill)........................1.4

ACCESS

North end. From the Eldora Trailhead (L), ski west on the King Lake Trail (29), 2.6 miles to the Lost Lake Trail (33), and follow it 0.5 miles to its end at Lost Lake. A total distance of 3.1 miles.

South end. From the Eldora Ski Area Trailhead (M), ski the Jenny Creek Trail (35), 1.9 miles to the Guinn Mountain Trail (36), which is followed 2.1 miles to its end at the Arestua Hut. A total distance of 4.0 miles.

USAGE

Nearly unused.

SNOW CONDITIONS

Poor, the snow in the gully can be hard windslab and subject to avalanche. On top, some areas may be blown clear but where protected by trees, even the broad pipeline swath snowpack can be good.

WIND EXPOSURE

The route is very exposed to wind along the ridgetop.

GRADIENT

Very steep in the gully, moderate thereafter.

ROUTE DESCRIPTION

From the Lost Lake Trail (33) terminus at the north end of Lost Lake, follow a trail east of the lake along the low ridge to the saddle east of the south end of the lake. Climb southwest to find a road climbing steeply to the left. Follow this road to enter the gully at the level of a prominent mine dump at 0.4 miles. Climb 600 feet up the steep curving gully to the level windswept flat atop the Guinn Mountain-Bryan Mountain ridge. Continue west, passing south of peak

10,918 on a climbing traverse to find the natural gas pipeline, a 20 yard wide swath cut through the trees, that follows the ridgeline west.

Ski the pipeline to the west end of a wide saddle from where the ridge can be seen to climb westward continuously to the summit of Guinn Mountain. The remnant of a small log cabin at the north side of the pipeline swath is here but may be buried in deep snow.

The Arestua Hut which marks the end of this route at 2.1 miles is visible to the keen-eyed from here, about 100 yards to the south in the second clearing. Only the front peak of the roof is visible.

The hut is operated by the Boulder Group of the Colorado Mountain Club, is open to all, and is not locked. It can comfortably accommodate about eight persons and has a wood stove. The operation of other cooking stoves is not permitted because of the fire hazard they pose.

ADDITIONAL CONNECTING TRAIL INFORMATION

The south end connects with the Guinn Mountain Trail (36) and the Rollins Pass Route (45) at the Arestua Hut.

SPECIFIC SKILLS RECOMMENDED

Technical skiing
Expert.

Endurance
Strenuous.

Routefinding
Advanced.

VIEWS

From the ridge top, distant vistas to the south include James Peak and Pikes Peak. To the north are South Arapaho Peak, the Indian Peaks, Mt. Meeker and Longs Peak.

PRIVATE PROPERTY AND OTHER RESTRICTIONS

If the Arestua Hut is used overnight or for a rest stop, read and abide by the rules posted for its use so as to not endanger it by fire and to insure that it will be clean and usable for the next group.

❄ ❄ ❄

TRAIL NO. 34A

LOWER GULLY BRYAN MOUNTAIN ROUTE

TRAIL MAP: 13

SUMMARY

Descent of the North Gully of Bryan Mountain can be continued down the same steep gully to the valley floor near Hessie. Direct and quicker, it is more difficult than the alternate Lost Lake and King Lake Trails.

CLASSIFICATION: Difficult.

MAPS (USGS 7.5' quadrangles)

Nederland (C3)

ELEVATIONS (feet)

```
Starting....................................9940
Highest....................................9940
Cumulative gain ...........................0
Cumulative loss........................820
```

DISTANCE (miles, one way).......0.8

TIME (hours)

```
Outbound (downhill)....................0.5
Return (uphill) ............................1.0
```

ACCESS

South (upper) end. Most commonly one would reach this end by descending the North Gully Bryan Mountain Route (34), 1.7 miles from Arestua Hut to where it turns out of the gully at a prominent mine dump. A total distance of 5.7 miles from the Eldora Ski Area Trailhead (M).

South (upper) end. A shorter but less used route from the Eldora Trailhead (L) goes 2.6 miles west on the King Lake Trail (29), 0.5 miles to the end of the Lost Lake Trail (33), and 0.4 miles on the North Gully Bryan Mountain Route. A total distance of 3.5 miles.

North (lower) end. From the Eldora Trailhead (L), ski 1.5 miles west on the King Lake Trail (29) to an unmarked junction where the road switchbacks right.

USAGE

Nearly unused.

SNOW CONDITIONS

Excellent, once the shelter of the trees on this untracked north-facing slope is reached. The upper part can be hard windslab and subject to avalanche.

WIND EXPOSURE

While the upper part is exposed to the effect of wind, most of the route is protected by trees.

GRADIENT

Very steep in the upper part, decreasing to moderate in the lower.

ROUTE DESCRIPTION

From the prominent mine dump, descend the gully to the valley bottom, then continue north to intercept the King Lake Trail at 0.8 miles.

ADDITIONAL CONNECTING TRAIL INFORMATION

None.

SPECIFIC SKILLS RECOMMENDED

Technical skiing
Expert.

James Peak from near Yankee Doodle Lake

Endurance
Moderate.

Routefinding
Intermediate.

VIEWS

Hessie townsite is visible in the valley below.

PRIVATE PROPERTY AND OTHER RESTRICTIONS

Cabins on private property are passed in the valley bottom.

❄ ❄ ❄

TRAIL NO. 35

JENNY CREEK TRAIL

TRAIL MAPS: 17, 16, 12

SUMMARY

From the Eldora Ski Area this popular trail climbs a beginners downhill slope, winds among other downhill runs, and drops slightly on a long traverse across a tree covered but south-facing slope into Jenny Creek. The easily followed trail continues on a jeep road up the long valley on an easy gradient, then climbs moderately to Yankee Doodle Lake, nestled in a glacial cirque at timberline.

CLASSIFICATION: Moderate-difficult.

MAPS (USGS 7.5' quadrangles)

Nederland (C3)
East Portal (C2)

ELEVATIONS (feet)

Starting....................................9360
Highest....................................10720
Cumulative gain 1600
Cumulative loss.........................240

DISTANCE (miles, one way).......4.6

TIME (hours)

Outbound 2.5
Return 1.3

ACCESS

At the Eldora Ski Area Trailhead (M).

USAGE

Heavy at the lower end, decreasing to light at the upper.

SNOW CONDITIONS

Good overall but variable. The beginners downhill slope has packed artificial snow. Snowpack on the trails through the ski area may show the effect of heavy usage. Although protected by trees, the descent into Jenny Creek is on a south-facing slope that can become icy from the heavy use and the effect of the sun. Meadows in the bottom of Jenny Creek can be bare, icy, and show exposed rocks. Beyond a 300 yard meadow at 2.4 miles the snowpack can be expected to be good to excellent until the open slopes below Yankee Doodle Lake are reached.

WIND EXPOSURE

The trail is generally well protected from wind by large trees except in a few clearings. The open slopes near Yankee Doodle Lake are exposed.

GRADIENT

Moderate slopes are climbed through the ski area. The descent into Jenny Creek can require good technique as the trail on the short moderate to steep gradient is narrow and can have poor snow. The valley bottom gradient is slight to 3.5 miles where the trail turns more northerly and climbs moderately to about 4.2 miles. After leveling out it then surmounts a final open moderate slope to the lake.

ROUTE DESCRIPTION

Climb the left side of the wide beginners downhill slope from the eastern parking lot and cross behind the top of the chair lift. Follow the *National Forest Access* and arrow signs on the maze of trails through the ski area to the blue diamond blazed, traversing descent into Jenny Creek and a sign-marked junction in a clearing with the Deadman Gulch Fee Trail (35A) at 1.6 miles.

Follow the jeep road west up Jenny Creek. Shortly past a third clearing, a post at 1.9 miles marks a junction with the Guinn Mountain Trail (36). Follow the unblazed left fork up the bottom of the valley past the roofless remnant of a cabin at 3.2 miles.

At 3.5 miles the trail, here indistinct if untracked, turns right and climbs more steeply through widely-spaced large trees, following the right fork of the valley seemingly split by a treeless knoll. The trail becomes less distinct as the trees thin and diminish in size and the effect of the wind becomes more pronounced as the valley route curves northward. The trail generally stays within 20 yards of the drainage. As the slopes become more open, the location of the lake in the glacial cirque at 4.6 miles is apparent.

ADDITIONAL CONNECTING TRAIL INFORMATION

An unmarked and probably untracked junction with the East Antelope Ridge Trail (37C) to the south is at 1.8 miles, 220 yards to the west of the second clearing along Jenny Creek. An arrow, visible to westbound traffic, and a sign *Dead End,* visible to eastbound, identify the turn-off point. From here, it is 100 yards west to the Guinn Mountain Trail junction.

At a prominent curve to the south at 2.6 miles, the West Antelope Ridge Trail (37B) crosses a bridge over Jenny Creek which may not be recognizable because of snow bridging the creek. A disfigured Forest Service post *502* is a few yards to the east, two metal posts are 20 yards to the west. An unmarked and untracked junction with the South Fork Jenny Creek Route (43C) to the south is at 3.5 miles where the trail turns right to climb more steeply.

An unmarked indefinite junction with the Jenny Creek-Forest Lakes Route (43B) is at 4.2 miles before the final climb to Yankee Doodle Lake.

SPECIFIC SKILLS RECOMMENDED

Technical skiing
Intermediate.

Endurance
Strenuous.

Routefinding
Beginner.

VIEWS

South Arapaho Peak is in full view from the top of the beginner slope at the start of the trail.

The bare knoll traversed by the railroad grade as it crosses the head of Jenny Creek on its way from East Portal to Yankee Doodle Lake and Rollins Pass is visible straight ahead on the steep descent into Jenny Creek at about 1.4 miles. The Jenny Creek-Forest Lakes Route (43B) crosses the saddle behind this knoll enroute to East Portal.

From Yankee Doodle Lake, a road sign marking where the Rollins Pass Route (45) joins the railroad grade is visible high above on the ridge to the northwest. The trace of the railroad may be followed south to Needle Eye tunnel. Unnamed peaks on the corniced continental divide above Forest and Arapaho Lakes are to the southwest. Standing alone to the south, James Peak rises above the tundra slopes of Nebraska Hill.

PRIVATE PROPERTY AND OTHER RESTRICTIONS

Access through the ski area on the designated marked trail to national forest land was secured by negotiation with the Eldora Ski Corporation, the use of other trails requires a trail pass. No dogs are allowed on the trail through the ski area.

TRAIL NO. 35A, 35B

DEADMAN GULCH FEE TRAIL, JENNY CREEK LOOP TRAIL

TRAIL MAP: 17

SUMMARY

An alternative to the lower part of the Jenny Creek Trail in gaining access to Jenny Creek from the Eldora Ski Area, the Deadman Gulch Trail climbs and descends less, and avoids the not uncommon poor snow conditions on the south-facing slope of the other trail. It does however require an Eldora trail pass. The Jenny Creek Loop Trail makes a closed loop in the vicinity of the bend of Jenny Creek and connects the Antelope Creek trails to the south with Eldora Ski Area. This short easy loop is included on the trail map but not included in the following data. It also requires an Eldora trail pass.

CLASSIFICATION: Easy.

MAPS (USGS 7.5' quadrangles)

Nederland (C3)

ELEVATIONS (feet)

Starting.....................................9360
Highest.....................................9540
Cumulative gain 290
Cumulative loss 110

DISTANCE (miles, one way).......1.8

TIME (hours)

Outbound 0.9
Return 0.7

ACCESS

At Eldora Ski Area Trailhead (M).

USAGE

Heavy.

SNOW CONDITIONS

Medium, nearly always well packed due to heavy use.

WIND EXPOSURE

Moderate.

GRADIENT

This alternate trail climbs the same moderate downhill slope as does the Jenny Creek Trail and descends a short moderate slope into Jenny Creek. Thereafter the trail up Jenny Creek is nearly flat.

ROUTE DESCRIPTION

Climb up the left side of the wide beginners downhill slope as for the Jenny Creek Trail (35). Cross behind the chairlift and turn left onto a narrow trail through the trees 20 yards from the lift. Turn right at a junction onto a road which descends through a sign-marked intersection to a wide meadow at the bend of Jenny Creek. Follow a jeep road up the valley, past a cable marking the private property boundary, to a junction with the Jenny Creek Trail (35), and the end of this trail at 1.8 miles.

ADDITIONAL CONNECTING TRAIL INFORMATION

From the confluence of Deadman Gulch with Jenny Creek at 0.8 miles west to a well at 1.0 miles, the trail is coincident with the sign-marked Jenny Creek Loop Trail (35B) which makes a closed loop in the vicinity of the bend of Jenny Creek extending south 0.2 miles to the Antelope Creek Trail (37).

SPECIFIC SKILLS RECOMMENDED

Technical skiing
Novice.

Endurance
Very easy.

Routefinding
Novice.

VIEWS

None.

PRIVATE PROPERTY AND OTHER RESTRICTIONS

An Eldora Ski Area trail pass is required. Dogs are not allowed on the trail.

❄ ❄ ❄

TRAIL NO. 36

GUINN MOUNTAIN TRAIL

TRAIL MAPS: 17, 16, 12

SUMMARY

Challenging for intermediate skiers, long and steep enough to give a good workout for all but the hardiest, the trail climbs out of Jenny Creek onto the upper slopes of Guinn Mountain to end at the Colorado Mountain Club's Arestua Hut. Situated at near-optimum snow conditions of high altitude and the protection of tall trees, the hut is a favorite day and overnight shelter for up and down skiers as well as those continuing over Rollins Pass to Winter Park.

CLASSIFICATION: Difficult.

MAPS (USGS 7.5' quadrangles)

Nederland (C3)
East Portal (C2)

ELEVATIONS (feet)

Starting.....................................9640
Highest...................................10960
Cumulative gain 1320
Cumulative loss............................0

DISTANCE (miles, one way).......2.1

TIME (hours)

Outbound 1.5
Return 0.7

ACCESS

From the Eldora Ski Area (M), ski the Jenny Creek Trail (35), 1.9 miles to a trail junction marked by a post.

USAGE

Moderate.

SNOW CONDITIONS

Good on the lower section, excellent higher.

WIND EXPOSURE

The trail is generally well protected from wind by trees.

GRADIENT

Steep sections are interspaced with more moderate. The steepest sections are where 400 feet altitude is gained in the first half mile, the lower part of the gully at 1.0 miles, and the headwall 300 yards beyond the ruins of a large cabin at 1.4 miles.

Approaching Arestua Hut

ROUTE DESCRIPTION

The blue-diamond blazed and easily followed trail climbs moderately steeply for a half mile from the junction on the Jenny Creek Trail (35) before leveling out for another half mile. It then climbs steeply entering a gully and following its steep right side it passes the ruins of a large cabin at 1.4 miles and 10,540 feet altitude. Switchback as needed to climb the steep treeless slope at head of the gully 300 yards beyond the cabin. Turn left at the top and continue on a slight to moderate climb west through large trees. The trail here with only widely spaced blue diamond blazes is not easily followed if untracked.

The Arestua Hut at 2.1 miles and 10,960 feet altitude is visible 100 yards to the left front from where the trail enters a windswept clearing. It is operated by the Boulder Group of the Colorado Mountain Club and is open to all. It is not locked nor hosted, can comfortably sleep about eight persons, and has a wood burning stove. The operation of other cooking stoves is not permitted because of the fire hazard they pose.

In the event it is not possible to follow the trail above the steep head of the gully at 1.6 miles, a convenient landmark and route to the hut is provided by the natural gas pipeline that extends west from Eldora Ski Area along the ridge connecting Bryan Mountain, Point 10918, Guinn Mountain, and Rollins Pass.

The swath cut through the trees is 20 yards wide and follows the crest of the ridge. It can be reached by skiing north through the moderately spaced trees from anywhere above the head of the gully.

To find the hut from the pipeline, ski west on the pipeline swath to the west end of a wide saddle where the ridge can be seen to climb westward continuously to the summit of Guinn Mountain. The remnant of a small cabin at the north side of the pipeline swath may be visible here in the deep snow. The Arestua Hut is visible from here, about 100 yards to the south in the second clearing. Only the front peak of the roof is visible.

CONNECTIONS WITH OTHER TRAILS AND ROUTES

Connections with the North Gully Bryan Mountain Route (34), the Rollins Pass Route (45), and the Yankee Doodle Cutoff Route (36A) are at the Arestua Hut.

SPECIFIC SKILLS RECOMMENDED

Technical skiing
Intermediate.

Endurance
Strenuous.

Routefinding
Intermediate.

VIEWS

From the lower part of the trail, the Moffat Route can be seen to the south across Jenny Creek as it climbs a twisting course from East Portal to Rollins Pass.

PRIVATE PROPERTY AND OTHER RESTRICTIONS

Abide by the posted rules for the Arestua Hut so as to not endanger it by fire and to insure that it will be clean and usable for the next group.

❄ ❄ ❄

TRAIL NO. 36A

YANKEE DOODLE CUTOFF ROUTE

TRAIL MAPS: 12, 16

SUMMARY

This exciting off-trail route descends through widely spaced trees from the summit of Guinn Mountain to Yankee Doodle Lake at the head of Jenny Creek. The steep descent is best done with good snow.

CLASSIFICATION: Difficult.

MAPS (USGS 7.5' quadrangles)

East Portal (C2)

ELEVATIONS (feet)

Starting 11210
Highest 11210
Cumulative gain 0
Cumulative loss........................600

DISTANCE (miles, one way).......0.6

TIME (hours)

Outbound (downhill)....................0.4
Return (uphill) 0.8

ACCESS

North end, at Guinn Mountain summit. From Eldora Ski Area Trailhead (M), ski the Jenny Creek Trail (35) 1.9 miles, the Guinn Mountain Trail (36) 2.1 miles to the Arestua Hut, and the Rollins Pass Route (45) 0.4 miles to the Guinn Mountain summit. A total distance of 4.4 miles.

South end, on Jenny Creek 0.3 miles south of Yankee Doodle Lake. From Eldora Ski Area Trailhead (M), ski 4.3 miles west on the Jenny Creek Trail (35) to an unmarked and untracked junction.

USAGE

Nearly unused.

SNOW CONDITIONS

Medium, the open area near the top of Guinn Mountain can be wind slab or blown free of snow.

WIND EXPOSURE

Exposed to wind near the top, but protected by trees lower on the slope.

GRADIENT

Very steep, the gradient can be lessened by going further south.

ROUTE DESCRIPTION

From the summit of Guinn Mountain, ski south along the edge of the steep drop-off to find a gradient of your liking. Pick a route through the trees down the steep slope to Jenny Creek at 0.6 miles.

ADDITIONAL CONNECTING TRAIL INFORMATION

None.

SPECIFIC SKILLS RECOMMENDED

Technical skiing
Expert.

Endurance
Strenuous.

Routefinding
Advanced.

VIEWS

From the top of Guinn Mountain, South Arapaho Peak is visible to the north across the tributary valleys of Middle Boulder Creek. To the south, the corniced ridge of the continental divide at the head of South Boulder Creek leads south to James Peak. Needle Eye tunnel on the Moffat Route and the present day passenger car summer route to Rollins Pass is close at hand, across the cirque of Yankee Doodle Lake at the head of Jenny Creek.

PRIVATE PROPERTY AND OTHER RESTRICTIONS

None.

❄ ❄ ❄

TRAIL NO. 37

ANTELOPE CREEK TRAIL

TRAIL MAP: 17

SUMMARY

The Antelope Creek group of trails form a network centered on Antelope Creek but extending over Antelope Ridge to Jenny Creek and the fee trails of Eldora. They also reach south and west to the switchbacks and loops on the giants ladder of the Moffat Route. These sheltered, unblazed, intermediate trails with generally fine snow are almost unused except for this, the main trail along the north side of Antelope Creek.

The Antelope Creek Trail follows the creek upstream on a moderate climb through dense timber along the north bank from the confluence with Jenny Creek to end at the railroad grade.

CLASSIFICATION: Moderate-difficult.

MAPS (USGS 7.5' quadrangles)

Nederland (C3)

ELEVATIONS (feet)

Starting....................................9240
Highest....................................9970
Cumulative gain 730
Cumulative loss.............................0

DISTANCE (miles, one way).......1.8

TIME (hours)

Outbound (uphill) 1.2
Return (downhill).........................0.7

ACCESS

East end. From the Eldora Ski Area Trailhead (M), ski the Deadman Gulch Fee Trail (35A), 0.8 miles to a junction in a clearing at the bend of Jenny Creek with the Jenny Creek Loop Trail (35B). Ski this south along the creek 0.2 miles to an unmarked junction with the Antelope Creek Trail (37). A total distance of 1.0 miles.

West end. From the Eldora Ski Area Trailhead (M), ski the Jenny Creek Trail (35), 2.6 miles to an unmarked junction with the West Antelope Ridge Trail (37B). Ski this 1.1 miles to the end at a junction with both the Antelope Creek Trail and the Giants Ladder Railroad Grade (41). A total distance of 3.7 miles.

USAGE

Light.

SNOW CONDITIONS

Medium.

WIND EXPOSURE

None.

GRADIENT

Moderate.

ROUTE DESCRIPTION (East to West)

From the unmarked junction at the south end of the Jenny Creek Loop Trail (35B), ski south 0.2 mile along the creek and turn west on an unmarked trail up the north side of Antelope Creek. Pass a square wooden railroad water tank at 0.7 miles and continue the moderate climb through dense timber to the railroad grade at 1.8 miles.

ADDITIONAL CONNECTING TRAIL INFORMATION

An unmarked junction with the Ladora Trail (37D) is at 0.4 miles as the trail enters the canyon of Antelope Creek.

At 1.2 miles an unmarked junction with the East Antelope Ridge Trail (37C), descending from the north is reached. A three foot metal stake, 130 yards to the west marks a junction with a forty yard connecting trail across the creek to the South Antelope Creek Trail (37A).

Eastbound skiers may encounter difficulty in getting started on west end of the trail if it is untracked. From the Giants Ladder Railroad Grade (41), marked with a sign *Forest Service Road 149*, turn east at the sign *Forest Service Road 502*, and after 10 yards bear slightly to the right and downhill. The West Antelope Ridge Trail (37B) continues to the left on a nearly level course. It is Forest Service Road 502 and is the more distinct trail but is less likely to be tracked.

SPECIFIC SKILLS RECOMMENDED

Technical skiing
Intermediate.

Endurance
Easy.

Routefinding
Beginner, see the above instructions to locate the west end.

VIEWS

No distant views. The square wooden water tank at 0.7 miles is a relic of the Moffat Road.

PRIVATE PROPERTY AND OTHER RESTRICTIONS

Most of the trail is on private property in section 31. Look for posted signs.

❄ ❄ ❄

TRAIL NO. 37A

SOUTH ANTELOPE CREEK TRAIL

TRAIL MAP: 17

SUMMARY

From the first switchback on the Giants Ladder, this trail crosses the saddle above the collapsed Tunnel 31 on the Moffat Road, and contours into Antelope Creek. There, the south bank is followed upstream to reach the railroad grade again where it crosses the creek.

CLASSIFICATION: Moderate.

MAPS (USGS 7.5' quadrangles)

Nederland (C3)

ELEVATIONS (feet)

Starting.....................................9400
Highest.....................................9920
Cumulative gain 560
Cumulative loss...........................40

DISTANCE (miles, one way).......1.3

TIME (hours)

Outbound (westbound) 1.2
Return (eastbound) 0.9

ACCESS

East end. From the Giants Ladder Trailhead (P), ski 2.3 miles on the Giants Ladder Railroad Grade (41) to the first switchback.

West end. From the Eldora Ski Area Trailhead (M), ski 2.6 miles on the Jenny Creek Trail (35) to an unmarked junction with the West Antelope Ridge Trail (37B), which is followed to its end at the railroad grade at 1.1 miles. A total distance of 3.7 miles.

The west end may also be reached from the Giants Ladder Trailhead (P), by skiing 5.3 miles on the Giants Ladder Railroad Grade (41).

USAGE

Nearly unused.

SNOW CONDITIONS

Medium on the south facing slope to the saddle at 0.3 miles, good thereafter on the north facing slopes of Antelope Creek.

WIND EXPOSURE

Well protected by dense trees except for the 300 yard clearing at the east end.

GRADIENT

Moderate, the steepest is a short climb to the saddle.

ROUTE DESCRIPTION

From the switchback at 2.3 miles on the Giants Ladder Railroad Grade (41), cross the 300 yard clearing to the north, passing above the ruins of the Zarlengo Cabin. A faint route climbs steeply just west of the collapsed tunnel toward the saddle. Near the top, a straight, better defined trail leads to the west, crosses the ridge, and continues on a near level course, now easily recognized, to reach the bottom of Antelope Creek further upstream.

The trail continues up the south side of the creek to a 100 yard clearing and immediately beyond, at 1.3 miles, the Giants Ladder Railroad Grade (41).

CONNECTIONS WITH OTHER TRAILS AND ROUTES

An unmarked junction with the Ladora Trail (37D), is at the Zarlengo Cabin ruins at 0.2 miles (300 yards).

At 0.8 miles an unmarked and easily missed junction with a 40 yard connecting trail across the creek to the Antelope Creek Trail (37) is passed.

SPECIFIC SKILLS RECOMMENDED

Technical skiing
Beginner.

Endurance
Easy.

Routefinding
Intermediate.

VIEWS

The collapsed remnant of Tunnel 31 on the Moffat Road is visible south of the saddle near mile 0.3.

The clearing at the west end of the trail is the site of Antelope station on the Moffat Road.

PRIVATE PROPERTY AND OTHER RESTRICTIONS

As with the Antelope Creek Trail, most of the trail is on the private property in section 31. Look for posted signs.

❄ ❄ ❄

TRAIL NO. 37B

WEST ANTELOPE RIDGE TRAIL

TRAIL MAP: 17

SUMMARY

A short easily followed jeep road on the good snow of a north-facing slope, it makes a gentle climb out of Jenny creek to cross the wind swept treeless ridge and contour into Antelope Creek and a common junction with both the railroad grade and the Antelope Creek Trail.

CLASSIFICATION: Moderate.

MAPS (USGS 7.5' quadrangles)

Nederland (C3)

ELEVATIONS (feet)

Starting....................................9820
Highest....................................9970
Cumulative gain 150
Cumulative loss...........................0

DISTANCE (miles, one way).......1.1

TIME (hours)

Outbound (southeast) 0.9
Return (northwest) 0.7

ACCESS

Northwest end. From the Eldora Ski Area Trailhead (M), ski the Jenny Creek Trail (35), 2.6 miles to an unmarked junction.

Southeast end. From the Giants Ladder Trailhead (P), ski the Giants Ladder Railroad Grade 5.3 miles to the end of that route as described here. This is marked with a road sign *Forest Service Road 502.*

USAGE

Very light.

SNOW CONDITIONS

Good.

WIND EXPOSURE

Protected by dense trees except at the ridge crossing.

GRADIENT

Nearly flat.

ROUTE DESCRIPTION

This jeep road ski trail is marked by post or sign at both ends as Forest Service Road 502.

From the disfigured Forest Service post *502* at the junction at mile 2.6 on the Jenny Creek Trail (35), cross the bridge over Jenny Creek which may not be readily recognizable because of snow bridging of the creek. Enter the trees on an easily recognized jeep road that traverses the side of the valley to the east southeast, climbing only slightly, to gain Antelope Ridge just below the tree cleared swath of the railroad grade.

Continue on a near-level course through a treeless area, re-enter the trees and continue below the railroad 400 yards on a distinct trail to the sign-marked junction at 1.1 miles with the railroad grade (Forest Service Road 149).

ADDITIONAL CONNECTING TRAIL INFORMATION

The end of the trail connects with both the Giants Ladder Railroad Grade (41), and with the Antelope Creek Trail (37). Recognition of this end of the Antelope Creek Trail can be difficult if untracked, a detailed description is given in that trail description.

SPECIFIC SKILLS RECOMMENDED

Technical skiing
Novice.

Endurance
Easy.

Routefinding
Beginner.

VIEWS

Bryan and Guinn Mountains are across Jenny Creek to the north.

PRIVATE PROPERTY AND OTHER RESTRICTIONS

None.

❄ ❄ ❄

TRAIL NO. 37C

EAST ANTELOPE RIDGE TRAIL

TRAIL MAP: 17

SUMMARY

Similar to the parallel West Antelope Ridge Trail, it is a short easily followed jeep road on the good snow of a north-facing slope. In the shelter of dense trees, it climbs gently out of Jenny creek to cross Antelope Ridge. It then contours into Antelope Creek and a junction near the midsection of the Antelope Creek Trail.

CLASSIFICATION: Moderate.

MAPS (USGS 7.5' quadrangles)

Nederland (C3)

ELEVATIONS (feet)

Starting.....................................9600
Highest.....................................9710
Cumulative gain.........................110
Cumulative loss...........................70

DISTANCE (miles, one way).......0.7

TIME (hours)

Outbound (southeast).................0.6
Return (northwest).....................0.5

ACCESS

Northwest end. From the Eldora Ski Area Trailhead (M), ski the Jenny Creek Trail (35), 1.8 miles to an unmarked junction.

Southeast end. From the Eldora Ski Area Trailhead (M), ski the Deadman Gulch Fee Trail (35A), 0.8 miles to a junction in a clearing at the bend of Jenny Creek, with the Jenny Creek Loop Trail (35B). Ski this south along the creek 0.2 miles to the unmarked junction with the Antelope Creek Trail (37). Follow this trail west 1.2 miles to an unmarked junction. A total distance of 2.2 miles.

USAGE

Nearly unused.

SNOW CONDITIONS

Good.

WIND EXPOSURE

Protected by dense trees.

GRADIENT

Slight.

ROUTE DESCRIPTION

From the unmarked junction at mile 1.8 on the Jenny Creek Trail (35), descend south about 40 feet in 100 yards on an indistinct route to cross Jenny Creek, then turn southeast to enter trees as the well defined trail climbs to the top of the ridge and descends the south side past a cable suspended on trees. It then switchbacks southwest and continues to an unmarked junction with the Antelope Creek Trail (37) at 0.7 miles.

ADDITIONAL CONNECTING TRAIL INFORMATION

The junction with the Jenny Creek Trail (35) is 220 yards west of the second clearing along Jenny Creek and 100 yards east of the junction with the Guinn Mountain Trail (36). An arrow, visible to westbound traffic on the Jenny Creek Trail, and a sign *Dead End,* visible to eastbound, identify the junction.

SPECIFIC SKILLS RECOMMENDED

Technical skiing
Novice.

Endurance
Easy.

Routefinding
Intermediate.

VIEWS

Bryan and Guinn Mountains are visible through the trees to the north across Jenny Creek.

PRIVATE PROPERTY AND OTHER RESTRICTIONS

None.

❄ ❄ ❄

TRAIL NO. 37D

LADORA TRAIL

TRAIL MAP: 17

SUMMARY

This is a short, low altitude connecting trail from Antelope Creek and the fee trails of Eldora Ski Area to the first switchback of the Giants Ladder of the Moffat Road.

CLASSIFICATION: Easy.

MAPS (USGS 7.5' quadrangles)

Nederland (C3)

ELEVATIONS (feet)

Starting.....................................9340
Highest.....................................9390
Cumulative gain 50
Cumulative loss.............................0

DISTANCE (miles, one way).......0.5

TIME (hours)

Outbound (southbound) 0.2
Return (northbound).....................0.2

ACCESS

North end. From the Eldora Ski Area Trailhead (M), ski the Deadman Gulch Fee Trail (35A), 0.8 miles to a junction in a clearing at the bend of Jenny Creek, with the Jenny Creek Loop Trail (35B). Ski this south along the creek 0.2 miles to the Antelope Creek Trail (37) which is skied 0.4 miles to an unmarked junction. A total distance of 1.4 miles.

South end. From the Giants Ladder Trailhead (P), ski the Giants Ladder Railroad Grade (41), 2.3 miles to the switchback. Ski the South Antelope Creek Trail (37A), 0.2 miles north across the clearing to an unmarked junction near the ruins of a cabin. A total distance of 2.5 miles.

USAGE

Light.

SNOW CONDITIONS

Poor at the exposed south end, good where protected by trees.

WIND EXPOSURE

Even at the treeless south end, the effect of wind is not excessive.

GRADIENT

Nearly flat.

ROUTE DESCRIPTION

From the unmarked junction at mile 0.4 on the Antelope Creek Trail (37), ski the easy near-level trail around the conical hill and across the meadow to the cabin ruins at 0.5 miles.

ADDITIONAL CONNECTING TRAIL INFORMATION

None.

SPECIFIC SKILLS RECOMMENDED

Technical skiing
Novice.

Endurance
Easy.

Routefinding
Beginner.

VIEWS

The cabin ruins at the south end mark the site of Ladora.

PRIVATE PROPERTY AND OTHER RESTRICTIONS

As with the Antelope Creek Trail (37) and the South Antelope Creek Trail (37A), the trail is on private property. Look for posted signs.

❊ ❊ ❊

TRAIL NO. 38

JENNY LIND GULCH TRAIL

TRAIL MAP: 17

SUMMARY

A short easy trail up the valley bottom, it gradually steepens enroute to a six hundred foot bowl where only an occasional tree restricts telemark descents of the moderate to steep slopes. Try to ski this bowl in midwinter or after a good snowfall as the relatively low altitude and exposure to sun and wind preclude consistently good snow conditions.

CLASSIFICATION: Moderate.

MAPS (USGS 7.5' quadrangles)

Nederland (C3)

ELEVATIONS (feet)

Starting.....................................8800
Highest....................................10470
Cumulative gain 1670
Cumulative loss............................0

DISTANCE (miles, one way).......2.6

TIME (hours)

Outbound 1.4
Return 1.0

ACCESS

At Jenny Lind Gulch Trailhead (N).

USAGE

Moderate.

SNOW CONDITIONS

Poor at the beginning, improving to medium in the bowl.

WIND EXPOSURE

Well protected by trees in the valley bottom, more exposed on the treeless slopes of the bowl.

GRADIENT

Steepness of the trail in the valley increases from nearly flat at the beginning to moderate. Slopes in the bowl are moderate to steep.

ROUTE DESCRIPTION

Jenny Lind bowl

From the small parking area at the trailhead on the Rollinsville-East Portal road, ski south up the valley bottom on the jeep road. Keep to the right at 300 yards where a posted road angles to the left. At 0.7 miles pass the first of three gullies draining into Jenny Lind Gulch from the west. The first in a 30 yard clearing is short, steep, brushy, and without a trail. The second gully at 1.0 miles is at the far end of a 150 yard clear corridor. Beyond here, the trail climb more steeply.

The valley and trail curve to the right to reach the bottom of the bowl at 2.2 miles. Climb 650 feet to reach the nearly level section of ridge at the top of the bowl at 10,470 feet and 2.6 miles.

ADDITIONAL CONNECTING TRAIL INFORMATION

The West Fork Loop Route (38A) branches from an unmarked junction to climb the second gully at 1.0 miles. The loop is completed at an indefinite junction on the ridge top at 2.6 miles.

At 1.4 miles, opposite the third gully, an alternative route, usually tracked, drops left and continues up the creek bottom paralleling the jeep road main route which climbs slightly onto the west side of the valley.

SPECIFIC SKILLS RECOMMENDED

Technical skiing
Intermediate overall. Novice at the beginning, intermediate to advanced in the bowl.

Endurance
Moderate.

Routefinding
Novice.

VIEWS

Abandoned mine workings on Dakota Hill are visible to the east.

PRIVATE PROPERTY AND OTHER RESTRICTIONS

None.

❄ ❄ ❄

TRAIL NO. 38A

WEST FORK LOOP ROUTE

TRAIL MAP: 17

SUMMARY

The route follows a short steep gully branching off from Jenny Lind Gulch and climbs 1300 feet to cross a ridge. Here the untracked expanse of the ski bowl at the head of Jenny Lind Gulch lies below.

CLASSIFICATION: Difficult.

MAPS (USGS 7.5' quadrangles)

Nederland (C3)

ELEVATIONS (feet)

Starting....................................9150
Highest....................................10470
Cumulative gain 1320
Cumulative loss............................0

DISTANCE (miles, one way).......1.6

TIME (hours)

Outbound (uphill) 1.5
Return (downhill)..........................1.0

ACCESS

From Jenny Lind Gulch Trailhead (N), ski 1.0 miles south on the Jenny Lind Gulch Trail (38) to an unmarked junction at the second gully from the right. This is at the far end of a 150 yard clear corridor.

USAGE

Nearly unused.

SNOW CONDITIONS

Medium.

WIND EXPOSURE

Protected from wind by the terrain until the ridge is approached.

GRADIENT

Very steep.

ROUTE DESCRIPTION

The route up this gully changes from a jeep road cut through trees at the bottom, to a wider open snow gully higher. It passes a mine dump at 9,920 feet. At 10,100 feet where the main gully curves slightly to the right, turn to the left and climb a smaller drainage up a moderately steep slope. Continue climbing south southeast through an area of thinned trees as the slope lessens to cross the ridge at 10,470 feet and 1.6 miles. This is the top of the bowl above Jenny Lind Gulch.

ADDITIONAL CONNECTING TRAIL INFORMATION

None.

SPECIFIC SKILLS RECOMMENDED

Technical skiing
Advanced.

Endurance
Moderate.

Routefinding
Advanced.

VIEWS

From the ridge top, the switchbacks of Giants Ladder on the Moffat Route, the downhill runs at Eldora Ski Area, and South Arapaho Peak are visible to the north across the valley of South Boulder Creek.

PRIVATE PROPERTY AND OTHER RESTRICTIONS

None.

❄ ❄ ❄

TRAIL NO. 39

BLACK CANYON TRAIL

TRAIL MAP: 17

SUMMARY

A little used trail up a low altitude forested north facing canyon, it is reached by a short cut-off route from Jenny Lind Gulch.

CLASSIFICATION: Moderate.

MAPS (USGS 7.5' quadrangles)

Nederland (C3)

ELEVATIONS (feet)

```
Starting...................................8840
Highest....................................9710
Cumulative gain .........................870
Cumulative loss............................0
```

DISTANCE (miles, one way).......2.3

TIME (hours)

```
Outbound ...................................1.9
Return .......................................1.2
```

ACCESS

From the Jenny Lind Gulch Trailhead (N), ski 200 yards up the Jenny Lind Gulch Trail (38), to an unmarked and probably untracked junction.

USAGE

Nearly unused.

SNOW CONDITIONS

Medium.

WIND EXPOSURE

Generally well protected by evergreen trees except for clearings and aspen groves in the creek bottom.

GRADIENT

Moderate.

ROUTE DESCRIPTION

From the unmarked junction on the Jenny Lind Gulch Trail (38), ski west across the stream on a level course near the base of the hill to the south. Continue to a barbed wire fence and staying on the left (south) side, follow it west to where a poorly defined jeep road can be seen heading up a shallow drainage to the left. Follow this jeep road past the several cabins and ruins of buildings including the old city hall that make up Baltimore at 0.6 miles.

From Baltimore, Black Canyon is visible up the drainage to the southwest. Pass three cabins about 300 yards beyond Baltimore on the right side of the creek and continue on the easily followed jeep road which stays on the right side of the creek, but sometimes climbs as much as a hundred feet above it. At 1.1 miles pass the weathered sign of the Henry Toll Ranch, *Toll Ranch 3,000 acres, 9,000 feet.*

At 1.5 miles the jeep road crosses the creek, then recrosses in 230 yards. At 1.7 miles the trail turns sharply to the right, away from the creek, to climb 50 feet in about 50 yards to pass a boiler and two cabin ruins. Above here the trail climbs a steep 80 feet, levels off and returns to creek level. Now more difficult to follow, it crosses the creek three times and ends in a 70 yard diameter clearing at 2.3 miles. A large dead tree draped with wire is near the center of this clearing.

CONNECTIONS WITH OTHER TRAILS AND ROUTES

The Baltimore Ridge Route (39A) continues on from the end of this trail.

SPECIFIC SKILLS RECOMMENDED

Technical skiing
Beginner.

Endurance
Moderate.

Routefinding
Intermediate.

VIEWS

None.

PRIVATE PROPERTY AND OTHER RESTRICTIONS

The trail is on the Henry Toll ranch. Private cabins are passed at Baltimore. Look for posted signs.

❄ ❄ ❄

TRAIL NO. 39A

BALTIMORE RIDGE ROUTE

TRAIL MAP: 17

SUMMARY

This unmarked route bushwhacks 550 feet up a timbered drainage from the end of the Black Canyon Trail to cross Baltimore Ridge and descend the open slopes to the Mammoth Gulch Road.

CLASSIFICATION: Difficult.

MAPS (USGS 7.5' quadrangles)

Nederland (C3)

ELEVATIONS (feet)

Starting....................................9710
Highest...................................10260
Cumulative gain 550
Cumulative loss.........................510

DISTANCE (miles, one way).......2.5

TIME (hours)

Outbound (westbound)...........2.0
Return (eastbound) 1.8

ACCESS

East end. From the Jenny Lind Gulch Trailhead (N), ski 200 yards on the Jenny Lind Gulch Trail (38), then 2.3 miles on the Black Canyon Trail (39) to its end.

West end. From the Tolland Trailhead (O), ski the Mammoth Gulch Road (40) 1.6 miles to the sign-marked jeep road junction. Take the upper (toward Apex townsite) of the three choices.

USAGE

Nearly unused.

Windy conditions on Baltimore Ridge

SNOW CONDITIONS

Medium in Black Canyon, poor on the exposed west side of Baltimore Ridge.

WIND EXPOSURE

Protected by trees in Black Canyon, very exposed on the ridge and west side.

GRADIENT

Steep.

ROUTE DESCRIPTION

From the dead tree clearing at the end of the Black Canyon Trail (39), climb through the moderately spaced trees following the east fork of the drainage on an off-trail route to 10,000 feet altitude. Angle to the right to cross the knoll between the forks at 10,220 feet, and contour across the head of the west fork to Baltimore Ridge at 1.0 miles. Follow the jeep road down the open slope to a sign-marked junction with the Mammoth Gulch Road (40) at 2.5 miles.

ADDITIONAL CONNECTING TRAIL INFORMATION

None.

SPECIFIC SKILLS RECOMMENDED

Technical skiing
Advanced.

Endurance
Strenuous.

Routefinding
Advanced.

VIEWS

From the ridge, the rugged east face of James Peak (13,294) is at the head of Mammoth Gulch to the southwest. To the north, the giants ladder switchbacks on the Moffat Route traverse the slopes across South Boulder Creek, South Arapaho Peak is visible ten miles distant.

PRIVATE PROPERTY AND OTHER RESTRICTIONS

Access to the east end of this route is through the Toll Ranch. Look for posted signs.

❄ ❄ ❄

TRAIL NO. 40

MAMMOTH GULCH ROAD

TRAIL MAPS: 17, 20, 19

SUMMARY

The wide U-shaped glacial valley of Mammoth Gulch is followed from Tolland up its gently curving course toward its source at the rugged east face of James Peak.

CLASSIFICATION: Moderate.

MAPS (USGS 7.5' quadrangles)

East Portal (C2)
Nederland (C3)
Empire (D2)
Central City (D3)

ELEVATIONS (feet)

Starting....................................8920
Highest...................................10240
Cumulative gain 1420
Cumulative loss............................0

DISTANCE (miles, one way).......4.8

James Peak from near Yankee Doodle Lake

TIME (hours)

Outbound 2.5
Return 1.5

ACCESS

At Tolland Trailhead (O).

USAGE

Light.

SNOW CONDITIONS

Poor at lower part, good on the upper.

WIND EXPOSURE

Except for a tree protected section above 1.6 miles, the lower 2.4 miles is exposed to the wind.

GRADIENT

Below the junction at 1.6 miles the gradient is moderate, above it is generally slight.

ROUTE DESCRIPTION

Follow the obvious wide road as it climbs from Tolland on a steady diagonal course out of the valley of South Boulder Creek to the floor of the higher Mammoth Gulch. At a sign-marked junction of jeep roads at 1.6 miles take the middle of three choices (Forest Service Road 176). After a short passage through trees, the road enters an open area on a gentle climb. Follow the jeep road by maintaining the gentle climb and watch for posts marking the road and for road cuts.

At 2.4 miles enter the trees as the well-defined road climbs the valley on the south side. At 3.4 miles pass a cabin and steam boiler on the left side and a mine dump on the right. A cable is across the road here. At 3.8 miles pass a cabin on the right. At 4.1 miles a road with a sign *No Trespassing* branches left uphill to a mine.

A barbed wire fence, gate, and *No Trespassing* signs at 4.8 miles bar further travel on the road. A substantial two story building and outbuildings are about 150 yards beyond. The remains of an ore processing table are near the gate.

CONNECTIONS WITH OTHER TRAILS AND ROUTES

A junction with the Baltimore Ridge Route (39A) is at the sign-marked jeep road junction at 1.6 miles.

SPECIFIC SKILLS RECOMMENDED

Technical skiing
Beginner.

Endurance
Moderate.

Routefinding
Beginner.

VIEWS

From the clear area beyond 1.6 miles, South Arapaho Peak is visible to the north while the east face of James Peak is visible at the head of Mammoth Gulch.

PRIVATE PROPERTY AND OTHER RESTRICTIONS

Posted mining operations are at the end of the road and on a side road along the way.

❄ ❄ ❄

TRAIL NO. 41

GIANTS LADDER RAILROAD GRADE

TRAIL MAPS: 16, 17

SUMMARY

A low altitude link from East Portal to Antelope and Jenny Creeks, it can serve as an alternative to a car shuttle for a return from a high altitude traverse. It can easily be followed in darkness or poor visibility, and with a constant gradient of 0.8 percent the track can be fast when packed by snowmobiles.

CLASSIFICATION: Moderate.

MAPS (USGS 7.5' quadrangles)

East Portal (C2)
Nederland (C3)

ELEVATIONS (feet)

Starting....................................9190
Highest....................................9950
Cumulative gain 760
Cumulative loss.............................0

DISTANCE (miles, one way).......5.3

TIME (hours)

Outbound (northbound) 2.5
Return (southbound) 2.1

Giants Ladder

ACCESS

South end. At Giants Ladder Trailhead (P).

North end. From Eldora Ski Area Trailhead (M), ski Jenny Creek Trail (35) 2.6 miles to the West Antelope Ridge Trail (37 B), which is skied 1.1 miles to its end. A total distance of 3.7 miles.

USAGE

Light, mainly by snowmobiles.

SNOW CONDITIONS

Poor to medium, usually packed by snowmobiles.

WIND EXPOSURE

Much exposure due to the lack of protection from trees to the wide roadbed.

GRADIENT

Slight, a constant 0.8 percent.

ROUTE DESCRIPTION

From the trailhead on the Rollinsville-East Portal road, follow the wide railroad grade on a steady climb out of the valley. Switchback sharply at 2.3 miles and continue on the road to the crossing of Antelope Creek at 5.2 miles and 200 yards more to a jeep road junction marked with a sign *Forest Service Road 502* at 5.3 miles. Although the railroad grade continues west up Jenny Creek, this is the end of the route described here.

ADDITIONAL CONNECTING TRAIL INFORMATION

An unmarked junction with the South Antelope Creek Trail (37A) is at the switchback at 2.3 miles.

A junction with both the Antelope Creek Trail (37), and the West Antelope Ridge Trail (37B), is at the road sign at 5.3 miles.

SPECIFIC SKILLS RECOMMENDED

Technical skiing
Novice.

Endurance
Easy.

Routefinding
Novice.

VIEWS

From the switchbacks, one can look across South Boulder Creek and up Mammoth Gulch. James Peak is to the right, behind the long ridge of Nebraska Hill.

PRIVATE PROPERTY AND OTHER RESTRICTIONS

None.

❄ ❄ ❄

TRAIL NO. 42

SOUTH BOULDER CREEK TRAIL

TRAIL MAPS: 16, 19

SUMMARY

One of the more popular trails in the area, it climbs 1900 feet from East Portal in little over three and a half miles to end near the timberline site of the former CMC Pfiffner Hut at Rogers Pass Lake. Almost the entire trail is in the shelter of tall trees, the snow is excellent, and the gradient steep enough for a rapid and interesting descent. One route branches off along the way and three others continue beyond the end of this trail to gain access to the ridge top and continental divide. From there, one can continue to Winter Park or descend another route on a high altitude loop tour.

CLASSIFICATION: Difficult.

MAPS (USGS 7.5' quadrangles)

East Portal (C2)
Empire (D2)

ELEVATIONS (feet)

Starting.....................................9210
Highest 11100
Cumulative gain 1890
Cumulative loss............................0

James Peak from slopes above Iceberg Lakes

DISTANCE (miles, one way).......3.6

TIME (hours)

Outbound 2.8
Return 1.4

ACCESS

At East Portal Trailhead (Q).

USAGE

Usage for the first mile is moderate, it decreases to light thereafter.

SNOW CONDITIONS

Medium to good for the first mile, excellent thereafter.

WIND EXPOSURE

The terrifying winds which seem to continuously sweep the East Portal trailhead area are left behind on entering the shelter of the trees in a hundred yards. The trail is well sheltered by tall trees until the area of mixed clearings and scattered clumps of trees is reached above the steep headwall at 3.2 miles.

GRADIENT

The gradient is slight for the first mile and moderate to steep thereafter except for the very steep headwall at 3.2 miles.

ROUTE DESCRIPTION

Cross the railroad tracks near the Moffat Tunnel entrance and climb over a padlocked gate at the bridge over the concrete ditch. The trail into the shelter of trees is about 100 yards to the south across a meadow and near a small building constructed of railroad ties.

Ski past several ranch buildings on the obvious, near level trail to a sign-marked junction with the Forest Lakes Trail (43) at 1.0 miles in the second of two large clearings. Continue across the clearing, passing above the ruins of a log cabin, to again enter the trees on a well-defined, steeper trail.

The trail is generally easy to follow, but is marked only occasionally with arrow and skier symbol signs and flagging. In places it can be difficult to follow if untracked. It climbs the main, more southerly drainage rather than the tributary drainage followed by the summer trail shown on the USGS map. As it curves right to the west, it passes close under the steep rocky northern slopes of James Peak. After climbing a short steep headwall requiring switchbacks, more moderate and open slopes are reached.

The drainage is followed west across open windswept meadows to Rogers Pass Lake at the base of Haystack Mountain at 3.6 miles. In poor visibility avoid climbing above 11,100 feet and onto the slopes and gullies leading up Haystack Mountain.

The Pfiffner Hut of the Boulder Group of the Colorado Mountain Club, was located about 100 yards east of Rogers Pass Lake. It became unserviceable after many years of use and was removed in 1988.

ADDITIONAL CONNECTING TRAIL INFORMATION

An unmarked and untracked junction with the Clayton Lakes Route (42D) is at 1.9 miles.

The Rogers Pass (42A), Heart Lake (42B), and Iceberg Lake (42C) Routes continue from Rogers Pass Lake to separate crossings of the continental divide ridge.

SPECIFIC SKILLS RECOMMENDED

Technical skiing
Advanced.

Endurance
Strenuous.

Routefinding
Intermediate.

VIEWS

The slopes of massive James Peak tower above the trail as it curves to the west on nearing Rogers Pass. From Rogers Pass Lake the subsidiary peak of Haystack Mountain is immediately to the south. To the west, switchbacks climb the windblown slope to Rogers Pass.

PRIVATE PROPERTY AND OTHER RESTRICTIONS

The lower part of the trail crosses the Henry Toll Ranch. Access through the ranch has been allowed after having been closed for two years in the late 1970's.

Stay on the established trail where it passes through the Henry Toll Ranch.

❄ ❄ ❄

TRAIL NO. 42A

ROGERS PASS ROUTE

TRAIL MAP: 18

SUMMARY

The Rogers Pass, Heart Lake, Iceberg Lakes, and Clayton Lake Routes are all steep, above-timberline routes branching from the South Boulder Creek Trail above East Portal. After climbing to the crest of the continental divide ridge they descend the tundra slopes west to the Rollins Pass Route at Riflesight Notch. All are shorter than the Rollins Pass Route, thereby reducing the exposure to the wind for a divide crossing but are more difficult to ski and more exposed to possible avalanche.

The Rogers Pass Route is best done by carrying skies and hiking when the switchbacked trail above the lake is blown free of snow.

CLASSIFICATION: Very difficult.

MAPS (USGS 7.5' quadrangles)

East Portal (C2)
Empire (D2)

ELEVATIONS (feet)

Starting 11100
Highest 11910
Cumulative gain 910
Cumulative loss..........................900

DISTANCE (miles, one way).......3.2

TIME (hours)

Outbound (westbound) 2.2
Return (eastbound) 2.2

ACCESS

From the East Portal Trailhead (Q), ski the South Boulder Creek Trail (42), 3.6 miles to its end at Rogers Pass Lake.

USAGE

Nearly unused.

SNOW CONDITIONS

Poor, the route may be blown clear.

WIND EXPOSURE

The entire route is exposed to the high winds and blowing snow common above timberline.

GRADIENT

Very steep on east side, moderate on the west.

ROUTE DESCRIPTION

From Rogers Pass Lake hike up the switchbacks of the trail 900 feet to the pass at 11,910 feet and 1.0 miles. Follow the road north on an easy descending traverse of the tundra slope to the trestle at Riflesight Notch at 3.2 miles and 11,107 feet.

CONNECTIONS WITH OTHER TRAILS AND ROUTES

An unmarked above timberline junction with the Jim Creek Headwall Route (44) is at Rogers Pass.

SPECIFIC SKILLS RECOMMENDED

Technical skiing
Expert.

Endurance
Very strenuous.

Routefinding
Advanced.

VIEWS

The corniced ridge of the continental divide extends north to the Arapaho

Climbing over boulders to divide above Clayton Lake

Peaks. James Peak looms nearby to the south. In the west, the distant peaks of the Gore Range are on the horizon beyond the Williams Fork Mountains. The ski runs of Winter Park and Mary Jane, cut into the forested slopes beyond the Fraser Valley, are visible down Jim Creek.

PRIVATE PROPERTY AND OTHER RESTRICTIONS

None.

❄ ❄ ❄

TRAIL NO. 42B

HEART LAKE ROUTE

TRAIL MAP: 18

SUMMARY

Like the Rogers Pass, Iceberg Lakes, and Clayton Lake Routes, this is an above-timberline route branching from the South Boulder Creek Trail above East Portal. It climbs the steep east side of the continental divide and descends the tundra slope west to a junction with the Rollins Pass Route at Riflesight Notch. It is the most direct of the skiable routes above Rogers Pass Lake, ascending a steep ridge immediately north of Heart Lake.

CLASSIFICATION: Very difficult.

MAPS (USGS 7.5' quadrangles)

East Portal (C2)
Empire (D2)

ELEVATIONS (feet)

Starting 11100
Highest...................................12050
Cumulative gain 950
Cumulative loss.........................940

DISTANCE (miles, one way).......2.9

TIME (hours)

Outbound (westbound) 2.2
Return (eastbound) 2.2

ACCESS

From the East Portal Trailhead, ski the South Boulder Creek Trail (42), 3.6 miles to its end at Rogers Pass Lake.

USAGE

Nearly unused.

SNOW CONDITIONS

Poor, the east end of the ridge northeast of Heart Lake may be clear of snow and the slope up the east side of the divide medium. The slopes on the west side of the divide are likely to be wind sculptured.

WIND EXPOSURE

The entire route is exposed to the high winds and blowing snow common above timberline.

GRADIENT

Very steep on the east side, moderate on the west.

ROUTE DESCRIPTION

Winter Park, Mary Jane, and Riflesight Notch

From Rogers Pass Lake, ski north up the moderate, above- timberline slope to the bench of Heart Lake. Climb the steep eastern end of the ridge north of the lake which may be blown clear of snow. Follow the crest of this ridge west with little gain in altitude as it becomes more bench-like, steep on the south side.

179

Ascend the right side of the sharp ridge southwest to the divide at 1.1 miles and 12,050 feet.

Descend the tundra slope northwest to intercept the jeep road which can be followed to Riflesight Notch and a junction with the Rollins Pass Route (45) at 2.9 miles.

ADDITIONAL CONNECTING TRAIL INFORMATION

None.

SPECIFIC SKILLS RECOMMENDED

Technical skiing
Expert.

Endurance
Very strenuous.

Routefinding
Advanced.

VIEWS

Similar to those for the Rogers Pass Route (42A).

PRIVATE PROPERTY AND OTHER RESTRICTIONS

None.

❄ ❄ ❄

TRAIL NO. 42C

ICEBERG LAKES ROUTE

TRAIL MAP: 15

SUMMARY

Like the Rogers Pass , Heart Lake, and Clayton Lake Routes, this is an above-timberline route which continues on from the South Boulder Creek Trail above East Portal. All climb the steep east side of the continental divide and descend the tundra slope west to a junction with the Rollins Pass Route at Riflesight Notch.

This route follows the Heart Lake Route to ascend the ridge north of Heart Lake. It then crosses the wide basin to the north and ascends an easier ridge to the continental divide south of Iceberg Lakes.

CLASSIFICATION: Very difficult.

MAPS (USGS 7.5' quadrangles)

East Portal (C2)
Empire (D2)

ELEVATIONS (feet)

Starting 11100
Highest...................................12120
Cumulative gain 1020
Cumulative loss.......................1010

DISTANCE (miles, one way).......2.4

TIME (hours)

Outbound (westbound) 2.0
Return (eastbound) 2.0

Corniced ridge of continental divide above Iceberg Lakes

ACCESS

From the East Portal Trailhead, ski the South Boulder Creek Trail (42), 3.6 miles
to its end at Rogers Pass Lake.

USAGE

Nearly unused.

SNOW CONDITIONS

Poor, the east end of the ridge northeast of Heart Lake may be clear of snow, the basin medium, the ridge leading to the divide can be hard wind slab near the top, and the slopes on the west side wind scoured.

WIND EXPOSURE

The entire route is exposed to the high winds and blowing snow common above timberline.

GRADIENT

Very steep on the ascent of the ridges of the east side, slight to moderate in the basin, and moderate on the west side.

ROUTE DESCRIPTION

As for the Heart Lake Route, from Rogers Pass Lake ski north up the moderate, above-timberline slope to the bench of Heart Lake. Climb the steep eastern end of the ridge north of the lake which may be blown clear of snow. Depart from the Heart Lake Route here and cross the basin to the north without loosing any significant altitude. Continue north up the steepening but moderate slope to gain the top of a subsidiary east-west ridge. Follow this ridge west as it steepens to join the continental divide at 1.2 miles and 12,120 feet. Avoid the wind slab on the steep drop-off to the north.

Descend the tundra slope northwest to intercept the jeep road which can be followed to Riflesight Notch and a junction with the Rollins Pass Route (45) at 2.4 miles.

ADDITIONAL CONNECTING TRAIL INFORMATION

None.

SPECIFIC SKILLS RECOMMENDED

Technical skiing
Expert.

Endurance
Very strenuous.

Routefinding
Advanced.

VIEWS

In addition to those described for the Rogers Pass and Heart Lake Routes, the view of the cornices on the eastern side of the continental divide ridge above Iceberg Lakes is memorable.

PRIVATE PROPERTY AND OTHER RESTRICTIONS

None.

❊ ❊ ❊

TRAIL NO. 42D

CLAYTON LAKE ROUTE

TRAIL MAPS: Page 16, 15

SUMMARY

Like the Rogers Pass, Heart Lake, and Iceberg Lakes Routes, this is an above timberline route branching from the South Boulder Creek Trail above East Portal. All climb the steep east side of the continental divide and descend the tundra slope west to a junction with the Rollins Pass Route at Riflesight Notch. This route is by far the most direct, branching off the South Boulder Creek Route less than two miles from East Portal and crossing the divide nearly directly above Riflesight Notch. On its way it climbs steeply through forested slopes to timberline at Clayton Lakes, and up a moderate open route to a rocky ramp free of snow leading to the continental divide north of Iceberg Lakes.

CLASSIFICATION: Very difficult.

MAPS (USGS 7.5' quadrangles)

East Portal (C2)

ELEVATIONS (feet)

Starting.....................................10080
Highest 11950
Cumulative gain 1870
Cumulative loss.........................850

DISTANCE (miles, one way).......2.4

TIME (hours)

Outbound (westbound) 3.4
Return (eastbound) 2.8

ACCESS

From the East Portal Trailhead, ski the South Boulder Creek Trail (42), 1.9 miles to an unmarked and untracked junction at about 10,100 feet altitude. The location isn't possible to specify exactly as there are no landmarks and an altimeter reading is of limited usefulness due to the nearly level terrain in the vicinity.

The best indicator of the approximate location is the view through sparse trees of two steep rocky knobs uphill to the northwest.

USAGE

Nearly unused.

SNOW CONDITIONS

Good to excellent conditions usually exist in the trees leading to Clayton Lakes, hard windpacked snow can be expected above timberline on the slopes leading to the ramp. The ramp is likely to be blown free of snow, and the steep tundra slopes on the west side of the divide can be wind scoured or blown clear.

WIND EXPOSURE

Protected by trees as far as Clayton Lake, exposed thereafter.

GRADIENT

Very steep on the ascent through the trees to Clayton Lake, moderate to steep for the remainder of the climb to the divide. The descent to Riflesight Notch is steep.

ROUTE DESCRIPTION

Bushwhack northwest through trees on a steep route up into the gap between the two rocky knobs described in the section on access. Turn west at 10,400 feet and ascend a steep drainage to gain a bench above and north of Clayton Lake at 0.8 miles.

Climb west up the moderate slopes of the above-timberline bowl toward the gap in the cornice along the divide. It may be necessary to remove skies to ascend the final section as the fierce winds scour a ramp-like corridor free of snow to expose boulders underfoot. The divide at 1.7 miles is at 11,950 feet.
Descend directly down the fall line to Riflesight Notch at 2.4 miles.

ADDITIONAL CONNECTING TRAIL INFORMATION

None.

SPECIFIC SKILLS

RECOMMENDED

Technical skiing
Expert.

Endurance
Very strenuous.

Routefinding
Expert.

Ramp above Clayton Lake

VIEWS

James Peak dominates the skyline to the south; the Gore Range, Williams Fork Mountains, and the downhill ski runs of Winter Park and Mary Jane are visible to the west. As from the Heart Lake Route the view of the corniced ridge of the continental divide , this time from the north, is spectacular.

PRIVATE PROPERTY AND OTHER RESTRICTIONS

None.

❄ ❄ ❄

TRAIL NO. 43

FOREST LAKES TRAIL

TRAIL MAP: 16

SUMMARY

After switchbacking north from the South Boulder Creek Trail a mile above East Portal, this moderately steep unblazed trail climbs through stands of towering trees to Forest Lakes and then a steep two hundred feet more to the drainage divide of Jenny and South Boulder Creeks. The up and back trip makes a fine tour or with a car shuttle, one can continue north into the Jenny Creek drainage and on to Eldora Ski Area, a total distance of 9.3 miles.

CLASSIFICATION: Difficult.

Surveying the route (above Clayton Lake)

185

MAPS (USGS 7.5' quadrangles)

East Portal (C2)

ELEVATIONS (feet)

Starting....................................9590
Highest....................................10820
Cumulative gain 1230
Cumulative loss............................0

DISTANCE (miles, one way).......2.0

TIME (hours)

Outbound (uphill) 2.0
Return (downhill).........................0.9

ACCESS

South or lower end. From East Portal Trailhead (Q), ski 1.0 miles on the South Boulder Creek Trail (42) to a sign-marked junction.

North or upper end. From Eldora Ski Area Trailhead (M), ski 4.2 miles on the Jenny Creek Trail (35) to an unmarked and untracked junction with the Jenny Creek-Forest Lakes Route (43B). Ski this route 2.1 miles to its end. Total distance 6.3 miles.

USAGE

Light.

SNOW CONDITIONS

Excellent.

WIND EXPOSURE

Exposed only briefly while crossing the easternmost of the Forest Lakes.

GRADIENT

Moderate to the turn-off from Arapaho Creek at 1.2 miles except for a short steep section above the creek crossing. Beyond the turn-off, the gradient is steep and unrelenting with only a short respite at the lake before the final very steep 200 feet to the ridge top.

ROUTE DESCRIPTION

Switchback sharply to the right at a sign-marked junction in a clearing at mile 1.0 on the South Boulder Creek Trail (42) and begin a moderate climbing traverse to the north into the trees. At 0.7 miles, cross the Creek and climb a short steep section to enter the hanging tributary valley, Arapaho Creek.

At 1.2 miles and 10,040 feet altitude, (840 yards past the creek crossing) turn off what appears to be the main trail continuing up the valley bottom onto an unblazed and frequently untracked faint trail climbing to the right. Further on, the trail is marked by tree slashes as it climbs steadily, leveling out only when near the easternmost of the Forest Lakes at 1.8 miles and 10,630 feet altitude.
Pick a route north northeast past the lake 200 feet more up the steep slope to the watershed divide at 2.0 miles where the route ends.

A modification of the route, which can easily be done without intending to, climbs to the north northwest to cross the ridge 200 feet higher at the railroad grade loop. From here one can follow the lower railroad grade north 0.9 miles to Jenny Lake.

Lunch stop near Forest Lakes

ADDITIONAL CONNECTING TRAIL INFORMATION

The Arapaho Creek-Forest Lakes Gully Route (43A) branches off at mile 1.2 to continue up the valley bottom.

The north end of the trail joins the Arapaho Creek-Forest Lakes Gully Route (43A), the Jenny Creek-Forest Lakes Route (43B), and the South Fork Jenny Creek Route (43C), at an inexactly located junction on the ridge above Forest Lakes.

SPECIFIC SKILLS RECOMMENDED

Technical skiing
Advanced.

Endurance
Strenuous.

Routefinding
Advanced. The turn off at 1.2 miles has no apparent distinguishing characteristics. I resort to counting the number of uphill skiing paces (about 440 for me) from the creek crossing at 0.7 miles to be assured of locating it without a search.

VIEWS

The view to the south from above the lakes is dominated by the massive bulk of James Peak. The cirques on the continental divide above Forest and Arapaho Lakes form a spectacular curtain to the west.

PRIVATE PROPERTY AND OTHER RESTRICTIONS

None.

❄ ❄ ❄

TRAIL NO. 43A

ARAPAHO CREEK-FOREST LAKES GULLY ROUTE

TRAIL MAP: 16

SUMMARY

An alternate to the Forest Lakes Trail, it continues on the obvious trail up Arapaho Creek from where the Forest Lakes Trail turns to climb steeply up the forested hillside. At the head of the gentle valley, it climbs a steep open gully to Forest Lakes.

CLASSIFICATION: Difficult.

MAPS (USGS 7.5' quadrangles)

East Portal (C2)

ELEVATIONS (feet)

Starting................................10120
Highest................................10820
Cumulative gain 700
Cumulative loss..............................0

DISTANCE (miles, one way).......1.3

TIME (hours)

Outbound (uphill) 1.2
Return (downhill)........................0.7

ACCESS

South or lower end. From East Portal Trailhead (Q), ski 1.0 miles on the South Boulder Creek Trail (42) to a sign-marked junction with the Forest Lakes Trail (43). Follow it 1.2 miles to where it climbs right from an unmarked junction. A total distance of 2.2 miles.

North or upper end. The access is identical to that for the north end of the Forest Lakes Trail (43). A total distance of 6.3 miles from Eldora Ski Area Trailhead (M).

USAGE

Light along the valley bottom, very light in the gully.

SNOW CONDITIONS

Excellent.

WIND EXPOSURE

Moderate.

GRADIENT

Slight along the valley bottom, very steep in the gully.

ROUTE DESCRIPTION

Continue on the obvious trail along the valley bottom from where the Forest Lakes Trail (43) turns off at an unmarked junction. The established trail ends in a steep-walled basin at 0.6 miles where a steep open gully descends the forested slope to the north. Climb the curving course of this gully to the middle Forest Lake at 0.9 miles. Climb northeast to cross the ridge as low as possible at 1.4 miles and 10,820 feet altitude.

ADDITIONAL CONNECTING TRAIL INFORMATION

The north end of the route joins the Forest Lakes Trail (43) the Jenny Creek-Forest Lakes Route (43B), and the South Fork Jenny Creek Route (43C) at an unmarked and only generally located junction on the ridge above Forest Lakes.

SPECIFIC SKILLS RECOMMENDED

Technical skiing
Advanced.

Endurance
Strenuous.

Routefinding
Advanced.

VIEWS

The corniced ridge of the continental divide above the glacial cirque settings of Arapaho and Forest Lakes is less than a mile to the west.

PRIVATE PROPERTY AND OTHER RESTRICTIONS

None.

❄ ❄ ❄

TRAIL NO. 43B

JENNY CREEK-FOREST LAKES ROUTE

TRAIL MAP: 16

SUMMARY

Heavily timbered slopes and the more open slopes of mixed clumps of stunted trees and meadows common at timberline are both traversed by this off-trail route. It connects Forest Lakes and the trails to East Portal with upper Jenny Creek and the trail to Eldora Ski Area.

CLASSIFICATION: Difficult.

MAPS (USGS 7.5' quadrangles)

East Portal (C2)
Nederland (C3)

ELEVATIONS (feet)

Starting....................................10820
Highest.....................................10820
Cumulative gain 20
Cumulative loss..........................220

DISTANCE (miles, one way).......2.1

TIME (hours)

Outbound (northbound)...............1.5
Return (southbound) 1.4

ACCESS

South end. From East Portal Trailhead (Q), ski 1.0 miles on the South Boulder Creek Trail (42) to a sign-marked junction with the Forest Lakes Trail (43). Follow it 2.0 miles to its end on the ridge above Forest Lakes. A total distance of 3.0 miles.

North end. From Eldora Ski Area Trailhead (M), ski 4.2 miles on the Jenny

Creek Trail (35) to an unmarked and untracked junction with the Jenny Creek-Forest Lakes Route (43B).

USAGE

Nearly unused.

SNOW CONDITIONS

Excellent.

WIND EXPOSURE

Exposed where the route skirts the open slopes of timberline.

GRADIENT

After a short moderate descent from the ridge, the traverse is near-level and ends with a moderate descent to Jenny Creek.

ROUTE DESCRIPTION

From the unmarked junction on the ridge above Forest Lakes, descend about 50 feet to more gentle terrain and traverse with only a slight loss of altitude across mixed open meadows and scattered clumps of trees to enter the continuous forest. Cross the saddle on the minor ridge dividing the forks of Jenny Creek and descend the moderate slope north to the curve of the railroad grade at its base.

Cross the valley bottom east northeast toward the treeless slopes of Guinn Mountain without gaining altitude to intercept the Jenny Creek Trail (35) at an unmarked and untracked junction at 2.1 miles.

ADDITIONAL CONNECTING TRAIL INFORMATION

The south end joins the Forest Lakes Trail (43) and the Arapaho Creek-Forest Lakes Gully Route (43A) from the south and the South Fork Jenny Creek Route (43C) from Jenny Creek; all at an unmarked and only generally located junction on the ridge above Forest Lakes.

SPECIFIC SKILLS RECOMMENDED

Technical skiing
Intermediate.

Endurance
Strenuous.

Routefinding
Advanced.

VIEWS

The route of the Moffat Railroad making its sinuous way across the head of Jenny Creek is visible on the tundra slopes toward the continental divide.

PRIVATE PROPERTY AND OTHER RESTRICTIONS

None.

❀ ❀ ❀

TRAIL NO. 43C

SOUTH FORK JENNY CREEK ROUTE

TRAIL MAP: 16

SUMMARY

An alternate to the Jenny Creek-Forest Lakes Route, it also connects Jenny Creek and the Eldora Ski Area with East Portal. Shorter and with good telemark skiing at the upper (southwest) end, one must bushwhack through dense timber in the creek bottom at the lower end.

CLASSIFICATION: Difficult.

MAPS (USGS 7.5' quadrangles)

East Portal (C2)
Nederland (C3)

ELEVATIONS (feet)

Starting..................................10820
Highest...................................10820
Cumulative gain 0
Cumulative loss.........................660

DISTANCE (miles, one way).......1.4

TIME (hours)

Outbound (northbound)...............1.0
Return (southbound) 0.8

ACCESS

Southwest end. From East Portal Trailhead (Q), ski 1.0 miles on the South Boulder Creek Trail (42) to a sign-marked junction with the Forest Lakes Trail (43). Follow it 2.0 miles to its end on the ridge above Forest Lakes. A total distance of 3.0 miles.

Northeast end. From Eldora Ski Area Trailhead (M), ski 3.5 miles on the Jenny

Creek Trail (35) to an unmarked junction with the Jenny Creek-Forest Lakes Route (43B).

USAGE

Nearly unused.

SNOW CONDITIONS

Excellent upper part, good lower.

WIND EXPOSURE

Moderate exposure on the higher open slopes, well protected lower in the trees.

GRADIENT

Moderate, the upper slopes offer good telemarking.

ROUTE DESCRIPTION

This description is for travel from the southwest to northeast. From the ridge above Forest Lakes, descend the fall line to the north through scattered clumps of trees and then continuous trees. Pick up an unmarked trail for a few hundred yards (an arm of the railroad "wye" turnaround) to cross the railroad grade as it curves to cross the creek at 0.8 miles .
Continue down through the thicket of dense small trees in the steep-walled drainage to about 10,200 feet where you are below the steep treeless knob crossed by the railroad grade to the north.

Bushwhack north across the near-level terrain to the Jenny Creek Trail (35) on the north side of the creek at 1.4 miles.

ADDITIONAL CONNECTING TRAIL INFORMATION

The southwest end joins the Forest Lakes Trail (43) and the Arapaho Creek-Forest Lakes Gully Route (43A) from the south and the Jenny Creek-Forest Lakes Route (43B) from Jenny Creek; all at an inexactly located junction on the ridge above Forest Lakes.

SPECIFIC SKILLS RECOMMENDED

Technical skiing
Advanced.

Endurance
Strenuous.

Routefinding
Advanced.

VIEWS

Distant views are shielded by the dense trees and terrain of the route except at the crossing of the railroad grade and on the open slopes near the upper end.

PRIVATE PROPERTY AND OTHER RESTRICTIONS

None.

❊ ❊ ❊

TRAIL NO. 44

JIM CREEK HEADWALL ROUTE

TRAIL MAPS: 18, 15, 14

SUMMARY

This is a very steep descent route from the continental divide near Rogers Pass into Jim Creek and on to Winter Park. It can be linked with the Rogers Pass, Heart Lake, or Iceberg Lakes Routes for a divide crossing from East Portal. The two thousand foot descent of open slope at the head of Jim Creek should not be attempted unless snow conditions are stable.

CLASSIFICATION: Very difficult.

MAPS (USGS 7.5' quadrangles)

East Portal (C2)
Empire (D2)
Fraser (C1)

ELEVATIONS (feet)

Starting 11860
Highest 11860
Cumulative gain 0
Cumulative loss.......................2760

DISTANCE (miles, one way).......3.8

TIME (hours)

Outbound (downhill)....................1.4
Return (uphill)........4.0 (not advised)

ACCESS

East or top end, on the continental divide. From the East Portal Trailhead, ski the South Boulder Creek Trail (42), 3.6 miles to its end at Rogers Pass Lake. Climb or ski either the Rogers Pass Route (42A) 1.0 miles, the Heart Lake Route (42 B) 1.1 miles, or the Iceberg Lakes Route 1.2 miles to the ridge top and continental divide. A total distance of 4.6 to 4.8 miles.

West or bottom end, at Jim Creek Trailhead, 0.4 miles south of Winter Park on Highway 40.

USAGE

Nearly unused.

SNOW CONDITIONS

Good conditions are likely on the steep open slope for the descent to Jim Creek. Excellent conditions should prevail for the remainder of the route.

WIND EXPOSURE

Exposed to wind on the steep open slope. Protected by trees thereafter.

GRADIENT

Very steep descent to Jim Creek, slight descent thereafter.

ROUTE DESCRIPTION

From the top of the continental divide, descend the very steep slope past scattered clumps of trees two thousand feet to the bottom of Jim Creek at 1.1 miles and 10,050 feet. Follow the jeep road trail down the valley to the highway at 3.8 miles.

ADDITIONAL CONNECTING TRAIL INFORMATION

None.

SPECIFIC SKILLS RECOMMENDED

Technical skiing
Expert.

Endurance
Very strenuous.

Routefinding
Advanced.

VIEWS

Similar to that from Rogers Pass Route (42A). The drop into Jim Creek is awesome.

PRIVATE PROPERTY AND OTHER RESTRICTIONS

None.

❄ ❄ ❄

Deep snow at Arestua Hut

TRAIL NO. 45

ROLLINS PASS ROUTE

TRAIL MAPS: 12, 16, 15, 14

SUMMARY

One of the classic routes of Front Range skiing, it crosses the continental divide at the historic Corona station site on Rollins Pass where the Moffat Railroad route once crossed prior to the 1928 completion of the Moffat tunnel. This is the easiest of the divide crossings from the eastern slope to Winter Park but has the longest exposure of about five miles, to the high winds and ground blizzards common above timberline.

An overnight stay at the Arestua Hut permits an early start on the crossing. The complexities of car shuttling can be avoided by using the metropolitan area RTD bus service from Denver or Boulder to Eldora Ski Area and returning from Winter Park village (Hideaway Park on USGS maps) to Denver by train or regularly scheduled bus service.

CLASSIFICATION: Difficult.

MAPS (USGS 7.5' quadrangles)

Fraser (C1)
East Portal (C2)
Nederland (C3)

Ridge above Yankee Doodle Lake

ELEVATIONS (feet)

Starting.................................10960
Highest.................................11760
Cumulative gain.......................910
Cumulative loss......................2770

DISTANCE (miles, one way).......9.2

TIME (hours)

Outbound (westbound)...............6.0
Return (eastbound)....................8.0

ACCESS

East end, at Arestua Hut. From Eldora Ski Area Trailhead (M), ski the Jenny Creek Trail (35), 1.9 miles to the Guinn Mountain Trail (36), and 2.1 miles to its end at the Arestua Hut. A total distance of 4.0 miles.

West end, at Winter Park Ski area.

USAGE

Very light.

SNOW CONDITIONS

Medium overall, the snow is generally good from the hut to the saddle above

Yankee Doodle Lake at 0.7 miles. The climb to the railroad grade at 0.9 miles is on hard windslab. The ridge leading to Rollins Pass and the descent to Riflesight Notch at 5.6 miles is all above timberline. Normally it has wind packed snow drifted into the road cut, however a significant part may be blown clear and walking may be necessary. It is important to have a pack with slots or some arrangement to carry skis.

The snow from Riflesight Notch to Winter Park, protected by trees, is frequently excellent.

WIND EXPOSURE

The five mile section above timberline is exposed to high winds out of the west and subsequent ground blizzards. Adequate clothing for extreme conditions, including face protection, is essential. The wind is less of a problem for eastbound travel.

GRADIENT

Generally moderate but with a steep climb from the saddle above Yankee Doodle Lake at 0.7 miles to the railroad grade, a steep descent of the South Fork of Ranch Creek where the route leaves the railroad grade below Riflesight Notch, and again where Buck Creek is followed in preference to the railroad at 7.4 miles.

ROUTE DESCRIPTION

From the Arestua Hut, climb the 250 feet to the top of Guinn Mountain at 0.4 miles, either by heading north to the pipeline swath and following it to the

Setting out for Rollins Pass from Arestua Hut

summit or by skiing uphill and west through a series of clearings. Ski west along the top of the narrow ridge above Yankee Doodle Lake and climb the wider steep wind-packed slope to the sign marking the railroad grade at 0.9 miles. Stay near the crest of the ridge to avoid the steeper slopes on either side that could avalanche.

Following the trace of a road if possible, climb the gentle tundra slope to the west. Stay on the north side and as much as 200 feet below the crest of the long ridge leading to Rollins Pass to avoid unnecessary climbing above the pass but at the same time keep high above the railroad trestles to avoid the steep side slopes above Middle Boulder Creek.

Rollins Pass on foot in near whiteout

From the gentle pass at 2.4 miles and 11,671 feet, follow the railroad grade on a steady descent of 4.5 percent to the south as it drops lower on the broad ridge of the divide. Telegraph poles are occasionally helpful to indicate the location of the railroad. Care should be taken in poor visibility to not mistake minor ridges to the west at BM 11382 and at the Corona Range Study Plot for the knob at Riflesight Notch. Riflesight Notch at 5.6 miles and 11,107 feet is identified by the railroad trestle.

Do not venture onto the trestle. Snow bridging large holes in the trestle could collapse under the weight of a skier.

Follow the road to the south from the top of the trestle and switchback north in 300 yards to arrive at the base of the trestle. With good snow conditions the steep descent from here of the South Fork of Ranch Creek is a delight. On reaching the railroad grade again in a level clearing at 6.8 miles, follow the wide roadbed on a near level course to where the slope changes so that the left side is downhill at 7.4 miles. Turn left off the road here down Buck Creek. Find the wagon road on the left side of the drainage, 0.7 miles and 400 feet below the turn off from the road. Follow the road down the drainage to the level aqueduct at 8.9 miles, turn right on it and go 500 yards to where a road downhill leads to Highway 40 and Winter Park ski area at 9.7 miles and 9100 feet.

ADDITIONAL CONNECTING TRAIL INFORMATION

The Upper Railroad Switchback Road (45A) branches off at the bottom of Riflesight Notch at 6.0 miles and rejoins the route at 6.8 miles.

The Lower Railroad Switchback Road (45B) continues on the railroad grade at 7.4 miles.

SPECIFIC SKILLS RECOMMENDED

Technical skiing
Advanced.

Endurance
Very strenuous.

Routefinding
Expert.

VIEWS

Outstanding views abound along the route. From Guinn Mountain, James Peak to the south and South Arapaho Peak to the north loom larger than all others. At the saddle at 0.7 miles, Yankee Doodle Lake is nestled in the bowl below at the head of Jenny Creek to the south while Middle Boulder Creek and the King Lake Trail are far below to the north. From Rollins Pass south, the distant sharp peaks of the Gore Range can be seen beyond Byres Peak and the Williams Fork Mountains. The downhill slopes of Winter Park and Mary Jane ski areas are across the Fraser Valley. If all other views are obscured by weather, the nearby rugged face of Mt. Epworth to the west can be seen in passing, about a mile south of Rollins Pass.

PRIVATE PROPERTY AND OTHER RESTRICTIONS

None.

❄ ❄ ❄

TRAIL NO. 45A

UPPER RAILROAD SWITCHBACK ROAD

TRAIL MAP: 15

SUMMARY

At times poor snow conditions for the steep descent of the South Fork of Ranch Creek below Riflesight Notch can be avoided by skiing the railroad grade switchback. Although much longer, the gentle gradient can be quite fast if packed by snowmobile traffic. Use of this alternate trail adds 2.4 miles to the Rollins Pass Route.

CLASSIFICATION: Moderate-difficult.

MAPS (USGS 7.5' quadrangles)

East Portal (C2)

ELEVATIONS (feet)

Starting 11100
Highest 11100
Cumulative gain 0
Cumulative loss........................800

DISTANCE (miles, one way).......3.2

TIME (hours)

Outbound (downhill)...................0.8
Return (uphill) 1.3

ACCESS

Upper end. At the bottom of Riflesight Notch, mile 6.0 on the Rollins Pass Route (45).

Lower end. At mile 6.8 on the Rollins Pass Route.

USAGE

Moderate.

SNOW CONDITIONS

Medium overall, the snow is generally packed by snowmobile traffic.

WIND EXPOSURE

The upper leg of the switchback is exposed to wind, the lower is less exposed.

GRADIENT

Constant and slight except moderate above the switchback at 1.6 miles.

ROUTE DESCRIPTION

From below the trestle at Riflesight Notch, ski the road west as it contours across the slope. Pass through a maze of snowmobile tracks near the ridge top at 0.7 miles and switchback sharply to the left at 1.6 miles after descending a steeper

Descent from Rifle Sight Notch

201

section. Follow the wide roadbed as it traverses back into the South Fork of Ranch Creek to the junction at 3.2 miles with the Rollins Pass Route (45) at a clearing where the road turns to cross the creek.

ADDITIONAL CONNECTING TRAIL INFORMATION

None.

SPECIFIC SKILLS RECOMMENDED

Technical skiing
Novice.

Endurance
Strenuous because of the access.

Routefinding
Novice.

VIEWS

The trestle at Riflesight Notch is at the upper end of the route, Winter Park is visible to the west across the Fraser valley.

PRIVATE PROPERTY AND OTHER RESTRICTIONS

None.

❄ ❄ ❄

TRAIL NO. 45B

LOWER RAILROAD SWITCHBACK ROAD

TRAIL MAP: 15, 14

SUMMARY

As with the Upper Railroad Switchback Road, the off-trail route down the drainage, this time Buck Creek, can be bypassed by following the near level railroad grade on its long meandering route to Winter Park. The route adds 4.7 miles to the Rollins Pass Route, including the 0.6 mile on Highway 40.

Winter Park village (Hideaway Park on the USGS map) can be reached by a variation of the route through the Idlewild slopes.

CLASSIFICATION: Moderate.

MAPS (USGS 7.5' quadrangles)

Fraser (C1)
East Portal (C2)

ELEVATIONS (feet)

Starting................................10180
Highest.................................10180
Cumulative gain 0
Cumulative loss.......................1080

DISTANCE (miles, one way).......6.4

TIME (hours)

Outbound (downhill)....................2.0
Return (uphill) 2.5

ACCESS

Upper end. At mile 7.4 of the Rollins Pass Route (45).

Lower end. At a road junction on Highway 40, 0.6 miles north of Winter Park Ski Area.

USAGE

Moderate, used frequently by snowmobilers.

SNOW CONDITIONS

Medium, packed by snowmobilers.

WIND EXPOSURE

Moderate.

GRADIENT

Nearly flat.

ROUTE DESCRIPTION

Continue on the road at mile 7.4 of the Rollins Pass Route (45). At 2.6 miles go straight through the crossroads near section marker 9666, and on to the junction at 6.4 miles with Highway 40, 0.6 miles north of the ski area.

ADDITIONAL CONNECTING TRAIL INFORMATION

One can ski to the village of Winter Park (Hideaway Park on the USGS map) by turning off the Lower Railroad Switchback Road at mile 4.1 where it turns left or south near section corner 9427. This road is followed 2.0 miles, through the Idlewild Ski Area to Highway 40, 0.7 mile north of town.

SPECIFIC SKILLS RECOMMENDED

Technical skiing
Novice.

Endurance
Moderate.

Routefinding
Novice.

VIEWS

None.

PRIVATE PROPERTY AND OTHER RESTRICTIONS

None.

TRAIL SUMMARY TABLE

Trail No.	Trail Name	USGS Maps	Trail Maps	Dif Rt	Tec Ski	End Rt	Rt Fnd	Surv[a] Mtn
1	Sandbeach Lake	A3	3,2	4	3	4	4	4
2	Thunder Lake	A3,A2	3,2,1	4	4	5	3	4
2A	Calypso Cascades	A3	2	3	3	2	1	2
3	Allens Park-Pear R	A3,A2	3,2	5	3	5	4	4
4	Rock Creek	A3	6	3	2	3	2	2
4A	E.Ridge St.Vrn Mtn	A3	5	4	4	5	4	5
5	St.Vrain Mtn	A3	6,5	4	4	4	3	4
5A	N.Gully St.Vrn Mtn	A3	5	5	5	5	4	5
6	Middle St.Vrain Rd	A3	6,5	2	1	3	1	1
7	Buchanan Pass	A3	6,5	3	2	3	2	2
7A	St.Vrain Glacier	A3,A2	5,4	4	2	5	4	5
8	Park Creek	A3	6	3	2	3	4	2
8A	Logging Road Spur	A3	6	2	2	1	2	2
8B	Rock Creek Saddle	A3	6	4	4	3	4	3
9	North Sourdough	A3,B3	6,8	3	3	2	2	2
9A	Beaver Res Cutoff	A3,B3	8	2	2	1	2	2
10	Coney Flats	A3,B3	8,6,5	2	2	3	2	3
10A	Four Wheel Drive	A3,B3	6,8,7,5	3	3	4	3	3
10B	Coney Flat-Mid SV	A3	5	3	2	4	2	3
11	South St.Vrain	B3,B4	9,8,7	3	3	4	3	2
11A	Chipmunk Gulch	B3,B4	9,8	1	1	1	1	1
12	Middle Sourdough	B3	8,7	3	3	4	3	3
12A	Beaver Res Road Ct	B3	8	1	1	1	1	1
12B	Church Camp Cutoff	B3	8	3	3	3	2	2
12C	Baptiste	B3	8	2	2	3	3	3
13	Waldrop (North)	B3	8,7	3	3	2	1	2
13A	Brainard Brdge Cut	B3	7	1	1	2	2	2
14	Brainard Lake Road	B3	8,7	1	1	1	1	1
14A	Brainard Lake Loop	B3	7	1	1	2	1	1
14B	Mitchell Lk Rd Spr	B3	7	1	1	2	1	1
14C	Long Lake Road Spr	B3	7	1	1	2	1	1
15	CMC South	B3	8,7	1	1	1	1	1
16	Little Raven	B3	8,7	3	3	2	1	2
17	Left Hand Park Res	B3	8	2	2	2	1	2
18	South Sourdough	B3	8,11	3	2	4	1	2
19	Niwot Ridge Road	B3	11	3	2	3	2	2
19A	Niwot Ridge Trav	B3	10,7,8	4	3	4	4	5
20	Mitchell-Blue Lake	B3,B2	7	4	3	4	3	4
21	Beaver Creek	B3,A3	7,5	5	5	5	5	5
21A	Audubon Cutoff	B3	7	5	4	5	5	5
21B	Firebreak Cutoff	B3	8,7	4	3	4	4	4
22	Pawnee Pass	B3,B2	7	3	3	4	2	3
23	Jean Lunning	B3,B2	7	3	1	3	3	2
24	Long Lake Cutoff	B3	7	2	2	3	3	2
25	Rainbow Lakes Road	B3	11,10	2	1	3	1	2

[a] see page 210 for unabbreviated column headings.

206

TRAIL SUMMARY TABLE

Mile Lnth	Hr Up	Hr Dn	Alt Gain	Alt Loss	Start Alt	Max Alt	Trl Head	Trl Type	Snow Qual	Amt Use	% Wind	Grad Av	Grad Max
4.2	3.2	1.7	2010	40	8360	10330	A	Tr	5	2	10	3	4
8.2	4.8	2.7	2400	120	8360	10760	A	Tr	5	3	2	3	3
1.5	0.7	0.5	570	0	9150	9720	A	Tr	2	1	0	3	3
5.8	3.4	2.0	1950	250	8900	10600	B	Tr	4	2	2	3	4
3.1	2.4	1.2	2100	0	8580	10680	C	Rd,Tr	3	3	2	4	3
1.5	1.2	0.8	650	130	10680	11330	C	Rt	3	1	70	3	4
3.5	3.0	1.4	2620	0	8580	11200	C	Tr	2	2	70	4	4
1.3	2.0	0.7	0	1100	11200	11200	C	Rt	4	1	5	5	5
4.7	2.0	1.5	1080	0	8520	9600	D	Rd	2	4	10	2	3
6.3	3.4	2.7	1390	0	8520	9910	D	Tr	2	3	10	2	3
2.7	2.4	1.2	990	0	9910	10900	D,E	JR,Rt	4	1	10	2	3
3.3	2.7	1.4	1200	0	8560	9760	D	JR,Tr,Rt	3	1	0	2	3
1.0	0.7	0.4	350	0	8870	9220	D	JR	2	1	5	2	3
1.8	1.5	1.5	380	420	9760	10140	D	Rt	2	1	7	4	3
1.6	1.3	1.0	540	0	8600	9160	D	Tr	3	2	0	3	4
0.8	0.6	0.4	0	270	9190	9190	E	Tr	3	1	2	2	3
3.2	1.9	1.3	600	0	9190	9790	E	JR	3	4	10	1	2
1.8	1.2	0.9	290	100	9590	9880	E	JR	4	1	0	2	3
0.6	0.5	0.3	30	230	9790	9820	E	JR	3	2	10	2	3
5.6	3.0	2.0	1730	70	8740	10480	G	Tr,JR,Tr	3	3	5	2	3
1.2	0.8	0.5	260	80	9190	9430	H	JR	2	2	10	1	2
6.3	3.5	3.1	600	1620	10060	10120	I,F	Tr	2	3	7	2	3
0.7	0.4	0.3	240	0	8920	9160	F	JR	1	1	10	2	2
0.3	0.3	0.2	80	0	9640	9720	G	Tr	2	1	0	3	3
1.0	1.0	1.0	80	80	9400	9440	F	Tr	3	1	0	1	1
2.8	1.4	1.0	510	230	10120	10420	I	Tr	3	4	5	2	3
0.5	0.3	0.3	80	40	10300	10380	I	Tr	4	2	10	1	1
2.1	1.2	1.0	290	50	10120	10360	I	Rd	2	5	90	1	1
1.0	0.5	0.5	40	40	10340	10370	R	Rd	2	5	70	1	1
0.4	0.2	0.2	110	0	10370	10480	R	Rd	3	5	70	1	1
0.4	0.2	0.2	130	0	10370	10500	R	Rd	2	5	70	1	1
2.2	1.0	0.8	360	60	10120	10420	I	Tr	4	5	5	1	2
2.7	1.5	0.9	540	200	10040	10580	I	Tr,Rd,Tr	4	3	7	2	4
1.7	1.0	0.6	550	0	10070	10620	I	Rd	2	4	50	2	3
5.5	3.1	2.5	450	1260	10060	10260	I,J	Tr	2	3	0	2	3
2.7	1.9	1.0	1200	0	9800	11000	J	Rd	3	3	30	3	3
2.4	2.0	1.7	440	840	11000	11440	J	Rt	2	1	100	3	4
2.3	1.7	1.0	840	0	10480	11320	R	Tr,Rt	5	3	30	3	3
4.4	4.0	3.8	820	1540	10500	11320	R	Tr,Rt,Tr	5	1	30	4	5
2.0	2.1	2.1	540	590	10450	10970	R	Rt	4	1	50	3	5
1.6	1.4	1.0	670	140	9360	10160	E	Rt	3	1	20	3	3
1.9	1.2	0.9	380	0	10500	10880	R	Tr	5	3	10	1	4
1.5	0.9	0.9	130	40	10520	10650	R	Tr	5	2	7	1	1
0.5	0.4	0.3	170	0	10360	10530	R	Tr	3	2	50	2	3
4.0	2.0	1.5	740	70	9290	9960	J	Rd	1	2	50	1	2

TRAIL SUMMARY TABLE

Trail No.	Trail Name	USGS Maps	Trail Maps	Dif Rt.	Tec Ski	End Rt.	Rt. fnd	Surv Mtn [a]
26	Glacier Rim	B3	10	4	3	5	3	5
26A	Rainbow Lakes Bowl	B3	10	4	5	5	4	5
27	Caribou Creek	B3,C3	11,10,13	2	1	2	2	3
28	Caribou Flat	C3	13	4	4	5	4	5
29	King Lake	C2,C3	13,12	4	2	5	3	4
30	Devils Thumb	C2,C3	13,12	5	5	5	4	5
30A	Jasper Creek	C2	12	5	5	5	4	5
31	Woodland Lake	C2	12	5	5	4	4	5
31A	Woodland Mt Overlk	C2	12	5	5	5	4	5
32	Fourth of July Rd	C2,C3,B2	13,12	3	2	3	1	2
33	Lost Lake	C3,C2	13	2	2	2	2	2
34	N.Gully Bryan Mtn	C3,C2	13,12	5	5	4	4	5
34A	Lower Gully	C3,C2	13	4	5	3	3	4
35	Jenny Creek	C3,C2	17,16,12	3	3	4	2	3
35A	Deadman Gulch,fee	C3	17	1	1	1	1	1
35B	Jenny Cr Loop,fee	C3	17	1	1	1	1	1
36	Guinn Mountain	C3,C2	17,16,12	4	3	4	3	4
36A	Yankee Doodle Cut	C3,C2	12,16	4	5	4	4	4
37	Antelope Creek	C3	17	3	3	2	2	2
37A	S.Antelope Creek	C3	17	2	2	2	3	2
37B	W.Antelope Ridge	C3	17	2	1	2	2	2
37C	E.Antelope Ridge	C3	17	2	1	2	3	2
37D	Ladora	C3	17	1	1	2	2	2
38	Jenny Lind Gulch	C3	17	2	2	3	1	1
38A	West Fork Loop	C3	17	4	4	3	4	4
39	Black Canyon	C3	17	2	2	3	3	2
39A	Baltimore Ridge	C3	17	4	4	4	4	4
40	Mammoth Gulch	C3,2;D3,2	17,20,19	2	2	3	2	2
41	Giants Ladder	C2,C3	16,17	2	1	2	1	2
42	S.Boulder Creek	C2,D2	16,19	4	4	4	3	4
42A	Rogers Pass	C2,C1,D2	18	5	5	5	4	5
42B	Heart Lake	C2,C1,D2	18	5	5	5	4	5
42C	Iceberg Lakes	C2,C1,D2	15	5	5	5	4	5
42D	Clayton Lake	C2,C1	16,15	5	5	5	5	5
43	Forest Lakes	C2	16	4	4	4	4	4
43A	Arapaho Cr-Frst Gl	C2	16	4	4	4	4	4
43B	Jenny Cr-Forest Lk	C2	16	4	3	4	4	4
43C	S.Fork Jenny Creek	C2	16	4	4	4	4	5
44	Jim Creek Headwall	C2,C1,D2	18,15,14	5	5	5	4	5
45	Rollins Pass	C2,C1	12,16,15,14	4	3	5	5	5
45A	Upper RR Switchbck	C2	15	3	1	4	1	4
45B	Lower RR Switchbck	C1,C2	15,14	2	1	3	1	2

[a] see page 210 for unabbreviated column headings.

TRAIL SUMMARY TABLE

Mile Lnth	Hr Up	Hr Dn	Alt Gain	Alt Loss	Start Alt	Max Alt	Trl Head	Trl Type	Snow Qual	Amt Use	% Wind	Grad Av	Grad Max
1.9	1.8	1.0	1070	0	9960	11030	J	Tr	5	1	7	3	3
1.9	2.0	1.7	0	1070	11030	11030	J	Rt	4	1	30	4	4
2.3	1.1	1.1	120	290	9990	9990	K,J	JR	1	1	90	1	1
2.6	2.2	1.7	1010	340	9320	10330	L,K	Rt	2	1	70	4	5
6.1	3.8	2.3	2090	0	8810	10900	L	JR,Tr,Rt	5	2	7	3	3
4.2	3.6	2.0	1660	0	9620	11280	L	Tr,Rt	5	2	15	3	5
2.2	1.7	0.8	0	990	11280	11280	L	Rt	5	2	20	3	4
1.9	1.7	1.2	1270	0	9710	10980	L	Tr,Rt	4	1	30	4	5
0.3	0.5	0.3	280	0	10980	11260	L	Rt	5	1	5	5	5
4.3	2.5	1.7	1170	0	8990	10160	L	Rd	3	4	30	2	3
0.5	0.5	0.3	160	0	9620	9780	L	Tr	3	2	30	2	2
2.1	2.0	1.4	1240	60	9780	10960	L	Rt	2	1	70	4	5
0.8	1.0	0.5	0	820	9940	9940	M	Rt	1	1	20	5	5
4.6	2.5	1.3	1600	240	9360	10720	M	Tr,Rt	4	5	5	2	4
1.8	0.9	0.7	290	110	9360	9540	M	Tr	3	5	10	2	3
0.8	0.3	0.3	0	0	9330	9330	M	Tr	3	5	50	1	1
2.1	1.5	0.7	1320	0	9640	10960	M	Tr	5	4	2	4	4
0.6	0.8	0.4	0	600	11210	11210	M	Rt	3	1	30	5	5
1.8	1.2	0.7	730	0	9240	9970	M	Tr	3	3	0	3	4
1.3	1.2	0.9	560	40	9400	9920	D	Tr	3	1	0	3	4
1.1	0.9	0.7	150	0	9820	9970	F	Tr	4	2	10	1	2
0.7	0.6	0.5	110	70	9600	9710	K,J	Tr	4	1	0	2	3
0.5	0.2	0.2	50	0	9340	9390	M	Tr	3	3	30	1	1
2.6	1.4	1.0	1670	0	8800	10470	N	Tr	2	4	30	3	5
1.6	1.5	1.0	1320	0	9150	10470	N	Tr,Rt	3	1	10	5	5
2.3	1.9	1.2	870	0	8840	9710	N	Rt,JR,Tr	3	1	5	3	3
2.5	2.0	1.8	550	510	9710	10260	N	Rt,JR	3	1	50	4	4
4.8	2.5	1.5	1420	0	8920	10340	O	Rd,JR	3	3	20	2	2
5.3	2.5	2.1	760	0	9190	9950	P	Rd	2	2	70	1	1
3.6	2.8	1.4	1890	0	9210	11100	Q	Tr	5	4	5	4	5
3.2	2.2	2.2	910	900	11100	11910	Q	Rt	2	1	100	4	5
2.9	2.2	2.2	950	940	11100	12050	Q	Rt	2	1	100	4	5
2.4	2.0	2.0	1020	1010	11100	12120	Q	Rt	2	1	100	5	5
2.4	3.4	2.8	1870	850	10080	11950	Q	Rt	3	1	100	5	5
2.0	2.0	0.9	1230	0	9590	10820	Q	Tr	5	3	3	4	4
1.3	1.0	0.7	700	0	10120	10820	Q	Tr,Rt	5	2	5	4	5
2.1	1.5	1.4	20	220	10820	10820	Q	Rt	5	1	20	2	3
1.4	1.0	0.8	0	660	10820	10820	Q	Rt	4	1	10	3	4
3.8	1.4	4.0	0	2760	11860	11860	Q	Rt,Tr	4	1	50	5	5
9.2	8.0	6.0	910	2770	10960	11760	M	Rt,JR,Rt	3	2	50	3	4
3.2	1.4	0.8	0	800	11100	11100	M	Rd	3	3	50	2	3
6.4	2.5	2.0	0	1080	10180	10180	R	Rd	3	4	30	2	2

COLUMN HEADINGS AND BRIEF
EXPLANATIONS FOR TRAIL SUMMARY TABLE

Col.

2   See *Contents* page i for full trail names.

3   See *Diagram* page 4 for USGS map names.

5   Column heading *Difficulty rating.*

6   Column heading *Technical skiing skill recommended.*

7   Column heading *Endurance rating.*

8   Column heading *Route-finding skill recommended.*

9   Column heading *Survival & mountaineering skill recommended.*

5-9   A rating of 5 means most difficult or highest level of skill. See *Index of trail characteristics* page 4 for conversion of numerical ratings to descriptive terms.

10   Column heading *Miles trail length.*

11   Column heading *Hours up.* Skiing time from trailhead to end. Trail description must be consulted to determine direction of travel on a few connecting trails.

12   Column heading *Hours down.* Skiing time for return.

13   Column heading *Altitude gain.* Cumulative, trail description must be consulted to determine direction of travel on a few connecting trails.

14   Column heading *Altitude loss.*

15   Column heading *Starting altitude.*

16   Column heading *Maximum altitude.*

17   Column heading *Trailhead.* See *Contents* page i for trailhead name or *Trailheads* page 17 for driving instructions.

18   Column heading *Trail type.* Rd=road, JR=jeep road, Tr=trail, Rt=route.

19   Column heading *Snow quality.* A rating of 5 means best snow.

20   Column heading *Amount of use.* A rating of 5 means most use.

21   Column heading *Percent wind.* Estimated percentage of trail exposed to wind.

22   Column heading *Gradient, average.* Gradient or steepness frequently encountered. A rating of 5 means steepest.

23   Column heading *Gradient, maximum.*

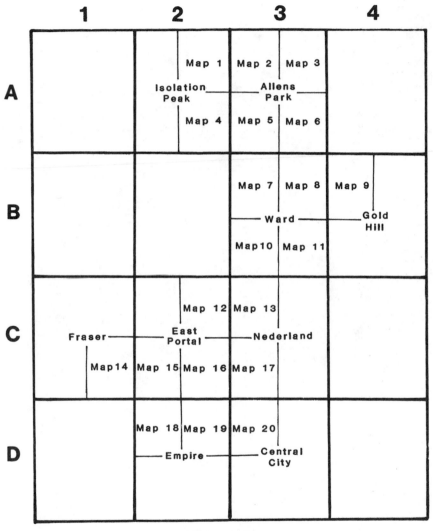

	1	2	3	4
A		Map 1 / Map 4 Isolation Peak	Map 2 / Map 3 Map 5 / Map 6 Allens Park	
B			Map 7 / Map 8 Map 10 / Map 11 Ward	Map 9 Gold Hill
C	Fraser	Map 12 East Portal Map 14 Map 15	Map 13 Nederland Map 16 Map 17	
D		Map 18 Map 19 Empire	Map 20 Central City	

Figure 4

Trail maps (numbered) shown on a mosaic of USGS
7.5 minute quadrangle maps. Each trail map is a quarter of a quadrangle.

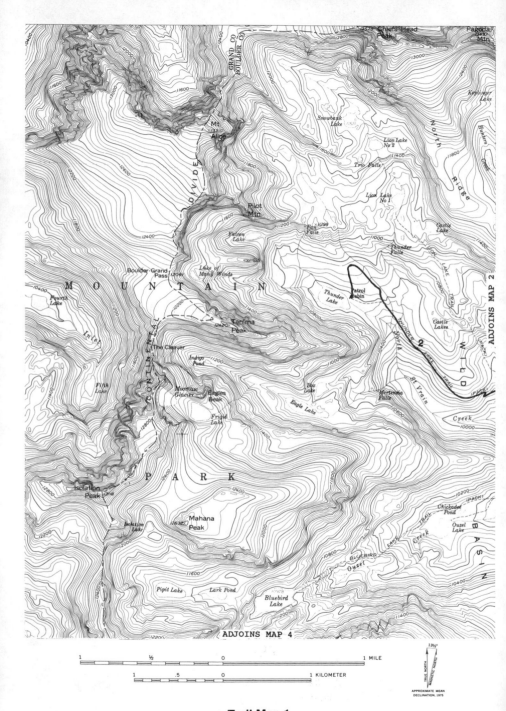

Trail Map 1
Northeast quarter of USGS Isolation Peak 7.5 minute quadrangle.

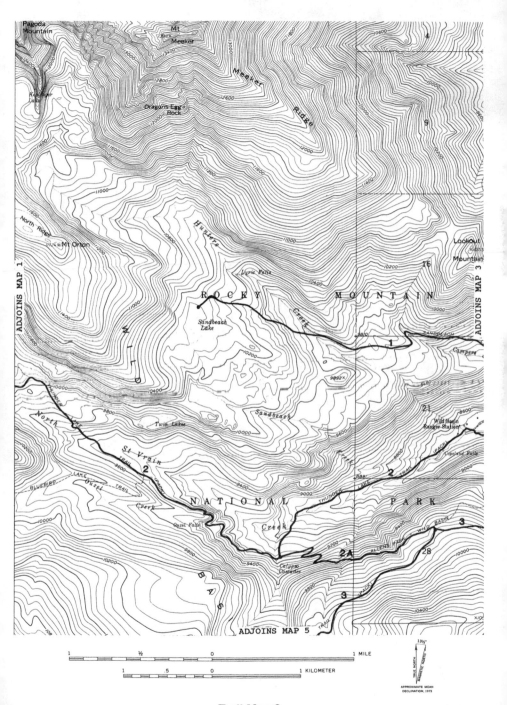

Trail Map 2

Northwest quarter of USGS Allens Park 7.5 minute quadrangle.

213

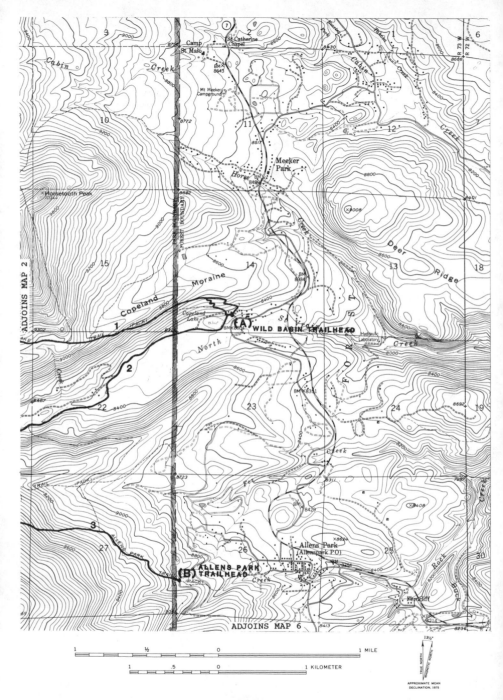

Trail Map 3
Northeast quarter of USGS Allens Park 7.5 minute quadrangle.

ADJOINS MAP 5

1   ½   0   1 MILE

1   5   0   1 KILOMETER

13½°

TRUE NORTH

MAGNETIC NORTH

APPROXIMATE MEAN
DECLINATION, 1975

Trail Map 4
Southeast quarter of USGS Isolation Peak 7.5 minute quadrangle.

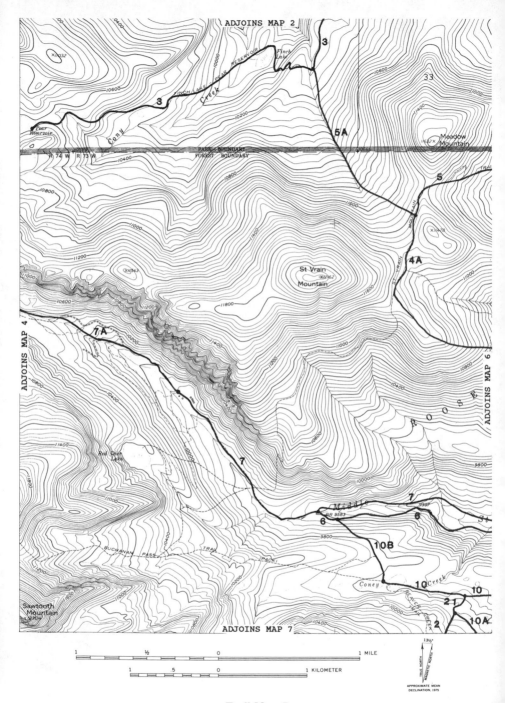

Trail Map 5
Southwest quarter of USGS Allens Park 7.5 minute quadrangle.

216

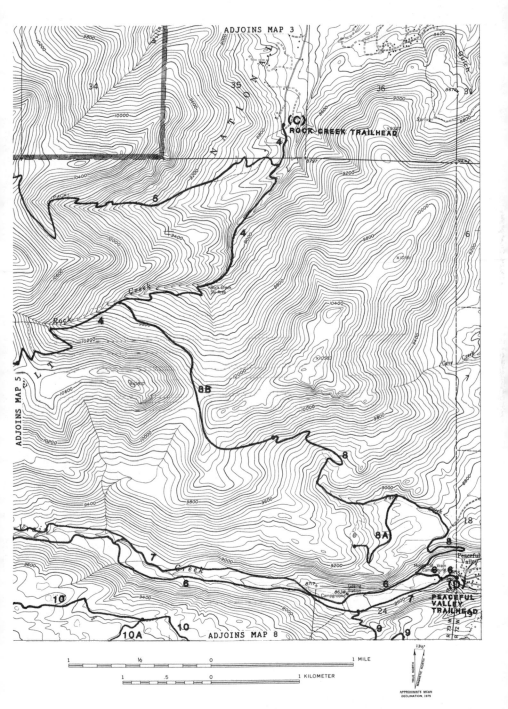

Trail Map 6

Southeast quarter of USGS Allens Park 7.5 minute quadrangle.

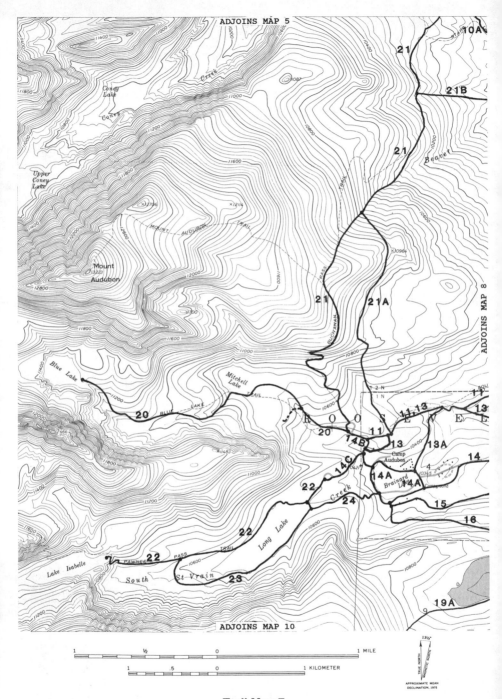

Trail Map 7

Northwest quarter of USGS Ward 7.5 minute quadrangle.

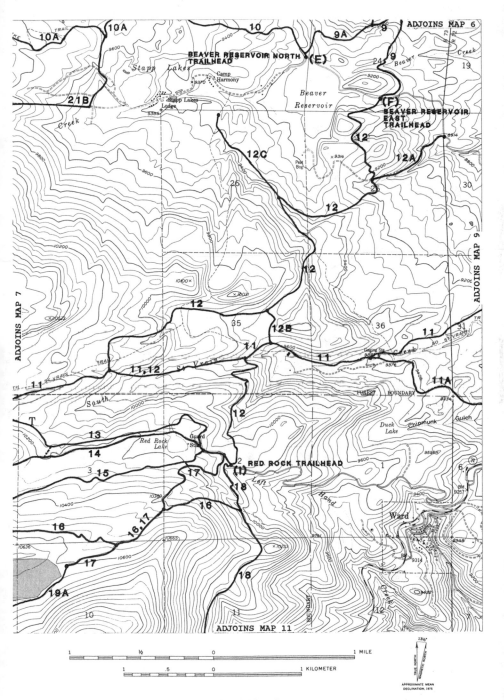

Trail Map 8
Northeast quarter of USGS Ward 7.5 minute quadrangle.

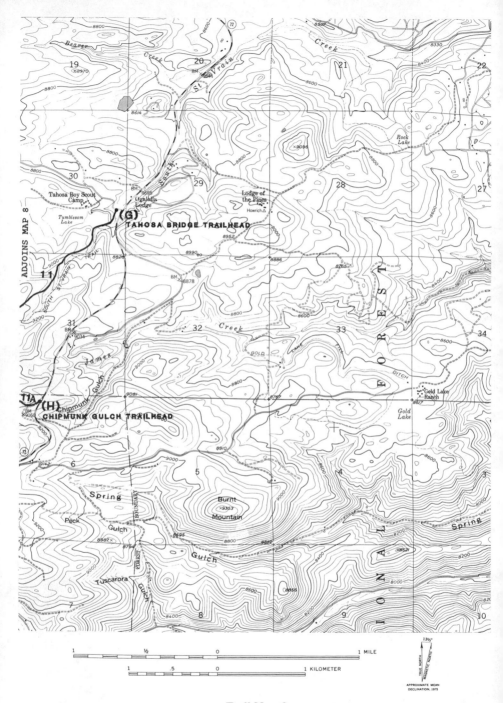

Trail Map 9

Northwest quarter of USGS Gold Hill 7.5 minute quadrangle.

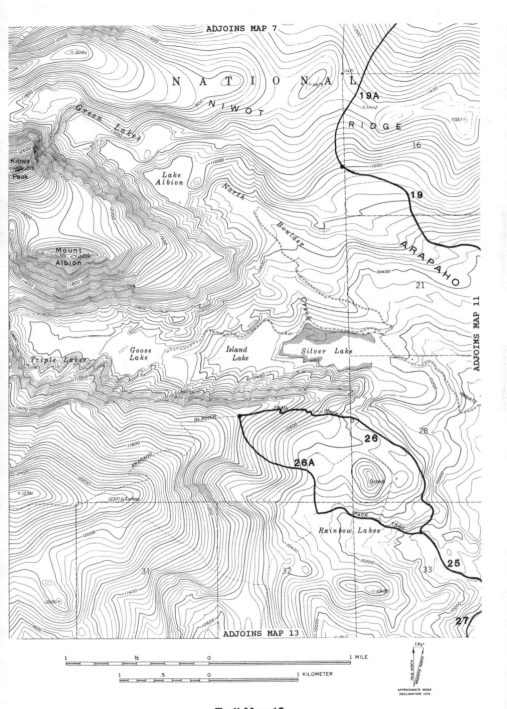

Trail Map 10
Southwest quarter of USGS Ward 7.5 minute quadrangle.

221

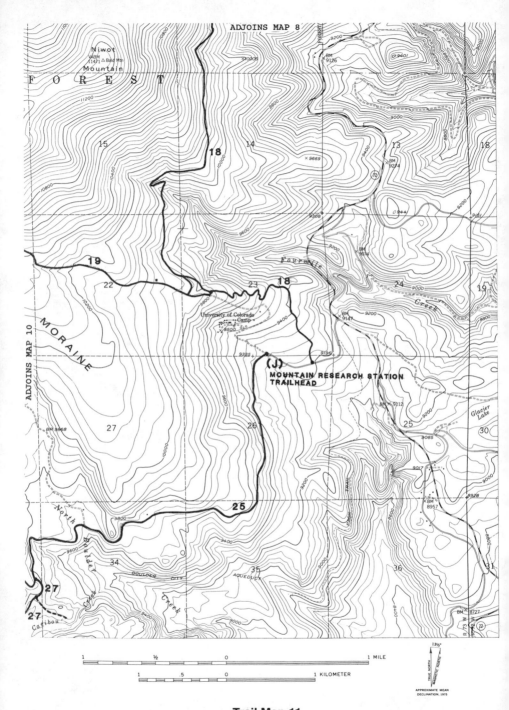

Trail Map 11
Southeast quarter of USGS Ward 7.5 minute quadrangle.

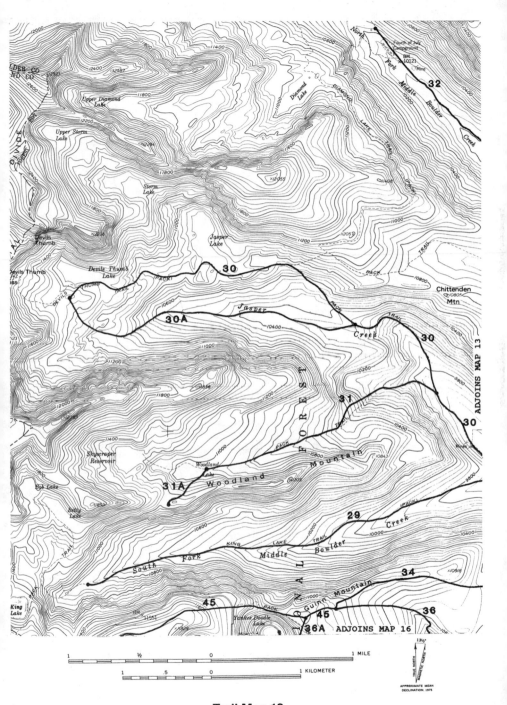

Trail Map 12

Northeast quarter of USGS East Portal 7.5 minute quadrangle.

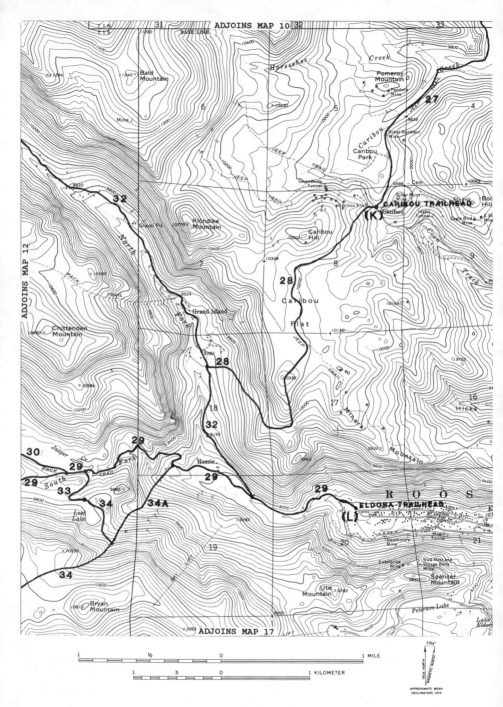

Trail Map 13

Northwest quarter of USGS Nederland 7.5 minute quadrangle.

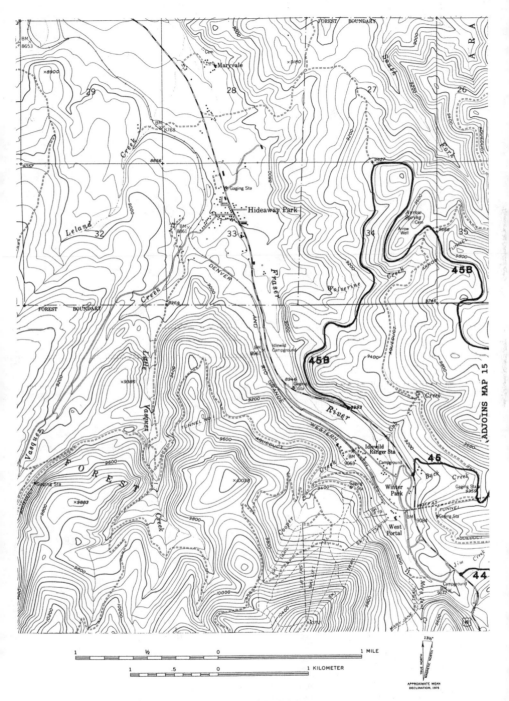

Trail Map 14
Southeast quarter of USGS Fraser 7.5 minute quadrangle.

225

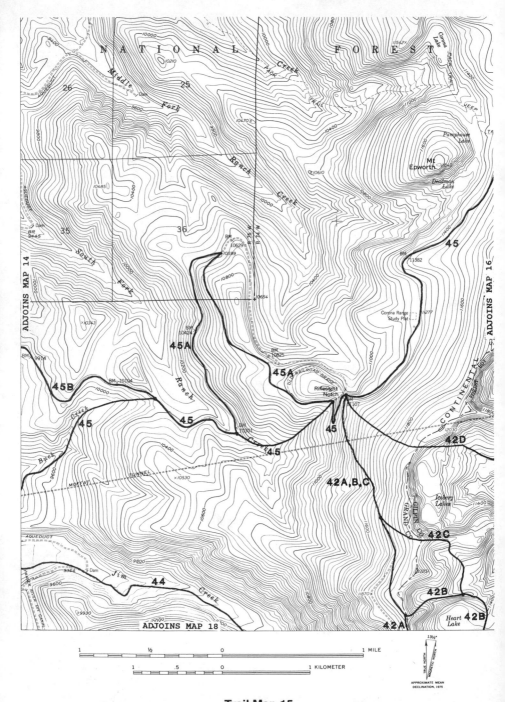

Trail Map 15

Southwest quarter of USGS East Portal 7.5 minute quadrangle.

226

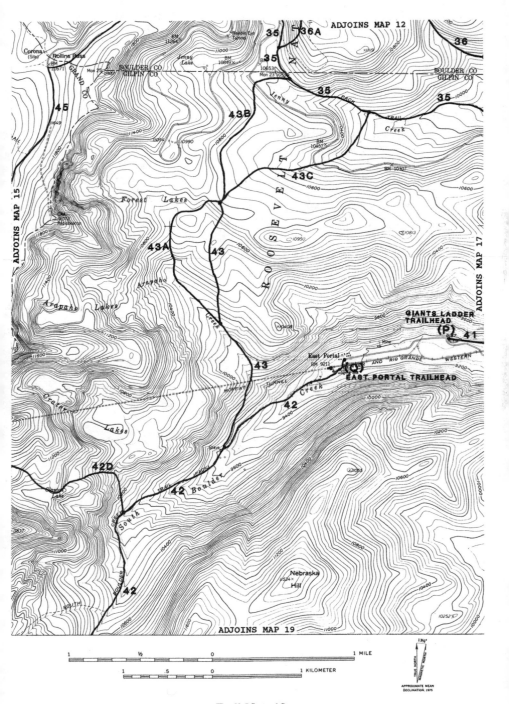

Trail Map 16
Southeast quarter of USGS East Portal 7.5 minute quadrangle.

227

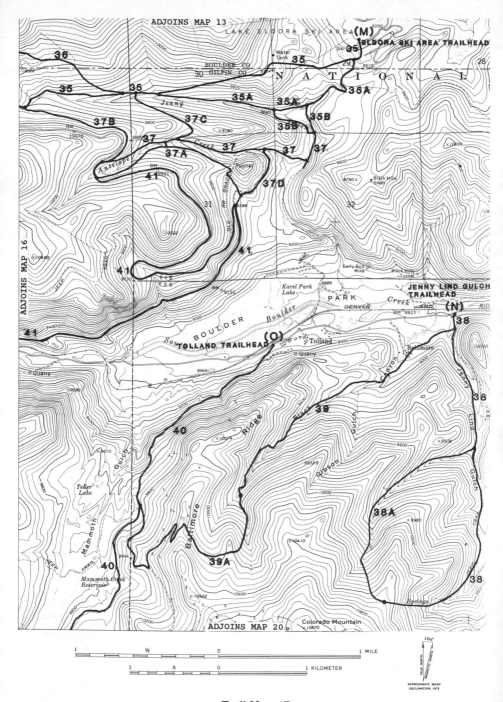

Trail Map 17

Southwest quarter of USGS Nederland 7.5 minute quadrangle.

Trail Map 18

Northwest quarter of USGS Empire 7.5 minute quadrangle.

229

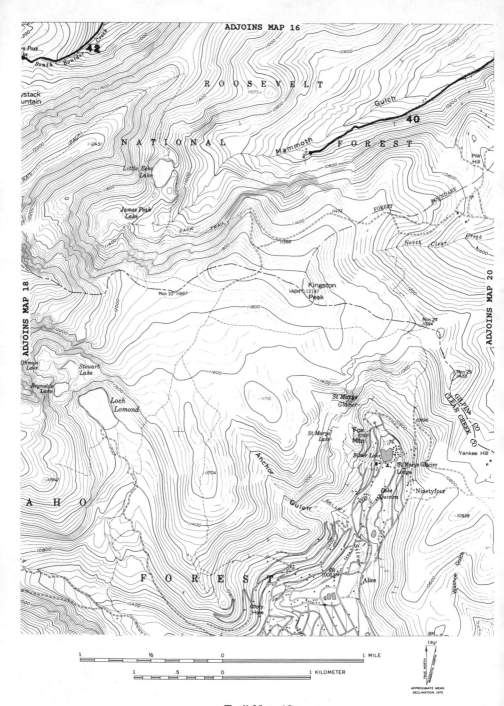

Trail Map 19

Northeast quarter of USGS Empire 7.5 minute quadrangle.

230

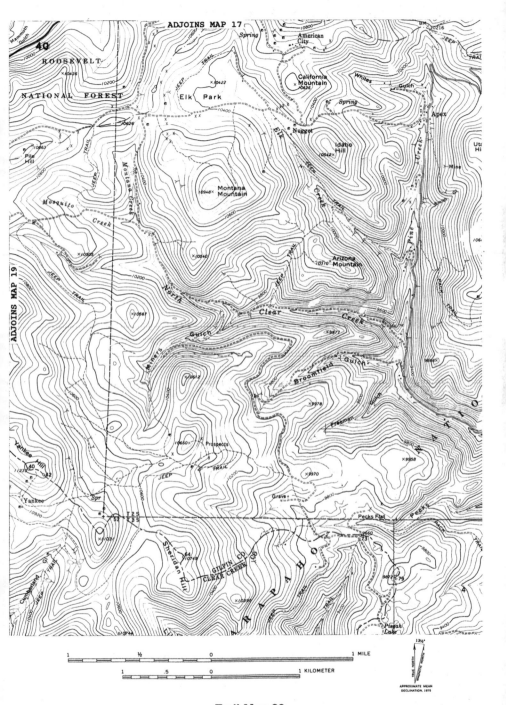

Trail Map 20

Northwest quarter of USGS Central City 7.5 minute quadrangle.

231

BIBLIOGRAPHY

Avalanche

The ABC of Avalanche Safety, E. R. LaChapelle, The Mountaineers

Avalanche Handbook, Agriculture Handbook 489, U. S. Department of Agriculture, Forest Service

The Avalanche Book, Betsy Armstrong & Knox Williams, Fulcrum Inc.

Ski Technique and Equipment

Mountain Skiing, Vic Bein, The Mountaineers

Backcountry Skiing, Lito Tejada-Flores, Sierra Club Books

Cross Country Skiing, Ned Gillette & John Dostal, The Mountaineers

Cross-Country Downhill, Steve Barnett, Pacific Search Press

Free-Heel Skiing, Paul Parker, Chesla Green Publishing Co.

The Telemark Movie, Dick Hall & John Fuller, North American Telemark Organization (70 minute videotape)

Cross-Country Ski Gear, Micheal Brady, The Mountaineers

Mountaineering

Mountaineering The Freedom of the Hills, Ed Peters Editor, The Mountaineers

First Aid

Medicine for Mountaineering, James A. Wilkerson, The Mountaineers

Advanced First Aid & Emergency Care, The American National Red Cross

Emergency Care and Transportation of the Sick and Injured, American Academy of Orthopaedic Surgeons

Hypothermia, Frostbite and other Cold Injuries, James A. Wilkerson, Cameron C. Bangs, and John S. Hayward, The Mountaineers

Hiking Trail Guidebooks

The Indian Peaks Wilderness Area Guide, J. Murray, Pruett

Rocky Mountain National Park Hiking Trails, K. & D. Dannen, East Woods

Colorado's Indian Peaks Wilderness Area-Classic Hikes and Climbs, Gerry Roach, Fulcrum

Fifty Front Range Hiking Trails, Richard DuMais, High Peak Books

Rocky Mountain National Park Trail Guide, E. Nilsson, Anderson World

Trails of the Front Range, L. Kenofer, Pruett

Skiing Guidebooks

Colorado Front Range Ski Tours, Tom and Sanse Sudduth, The Touchstone Press

Fifty Colorado Ski Tours, Richard Du Mais, High Peak Publishing

Ski Trail Map, Brainard Lake-Middle St Vrain, Harlan Barton, Colorado Mountain Club

Tree Identification

Rocky Mountain Tree Finder, Tom Watts, Nature Study Guild

Geology

Geology of National Parks, Ann Harris and Esther Tuttle, Kendall/Hunt

Roadside Geology of Colorado, Halka Chronic, Mountain Press

Prairie Peak and Plateau, John and Halka Chronic, Colorado Geological Survey Bulletin 32

A Guide to the Geology of the Boulder Region, P. G. Worcester, Boulder Chamber of Commerce

History

Red Rocks to Riches, Silvia Pettem, Stonehenge Books

Rails that Climb, Edward T. Bolinger, Colorado Railroad Historical Foundation

The Moffat Road, Edward T. Bolinger and Frederick Bauer, Sage Books

INDEX

ABOUT THE AUTHOR: Harlan Barton

A fascination with maps was first piqued as a field artillery forward observer during the Korean War. It continued later with the challenge of navigating low level helicopter flights while conducting geologic field work in remote areas of Alaska and the West. This has been combined with a long-standing enthusiasm for exploring new areas for cross country skiing to make him uniquely qualified to produce this comprehensive guide to cross country skiing on the eastern slope of the Front Range.

Living in Boulder, he is a trip leader for the Colorado Mountain Club and a past member of the Rocky Mountain Rescue Group. A ski trail map of the Brainard Lake and Middle St. Vrain area published by the Colorado Mountain Club is an earlier product of his mapping. As a geochemist with the U. S. Geological Survey, he has worked extensively in exploring the mineral resources of areas proposed for wilderness status. In addition to Colorado and adjacent states, he has hiked and climbed in Alaska, British Columbia, the Cascade and Sierra Nevada ranges, Mexico, South America, and Nepal.